CLASSIC fM

EVERYTHING YOU EVER
WANTED TO KNOW ABOUT
CLASSICAL MUSIC
BUT WERE TOO AFRAID TO ASK

CLASSIC *f*M

EVERYTHING YOU EVER WANTED TO KNOW ABOUT CLASSICAL MUSIC BUT WERE TOO AFRAID TO ASK

DARREN HENLEY AND SAM JACKSON

First published 2012
This paperback edition published in 2013 by
Elliott and Thompson Limited
27 John Street, London WC1N 2BX
www.eandtbooks.com

ISBN: 978-1-90965-383-2

Available as an ebook
epub 978-1-90764-250-0
mobi 978-1-90764-297-5
PDF 978-1-90764-298-2

Text © Darren Henley and Sam Jackson 2012

9 8 7 6 5 4 3 2 1

A CIP catalogue record for this book is available from the British Library.

Printed by CPI Group (UK) Ltd, Croydon, CR0 4YY

Typeset by Envy Design

global
RADIO

CONTENTS

INTRODUCTION

Classic FM is the UK's only 100 per cent classical music radio station. Since we began broadcasting 20 years ago in September 1992, the station has brought classical music to millions of people across the UK. If you've yet to discover for yourself the delights of being able to listen to the world's greatest music 24 hours a day, you can find Classic FM on 100–102 FM, on Digital Radio, online at www.classicfm.com, on Sky channel 0106, on Virgin Media channel 922 and on FreeSat channel 721.

As we're celebrating 20 years since we turned on our transmitters for the very first time, we thought that we would put together the guide to classical music that we would rather have liked to have produced for our new listeners when Classic FM began its life. Of course, we didn't know quite as much about classical music back then as we do now, given that we've been able to enjoy a further two decades of accumulated listening.

We've also learned a lot about what our listeners like to hear – as well as some of the music that they are a little less keen on. Since 1992, we've researched hundreds of weeks of programming and listened to the thousands of new recordings that arrive at our studios each year. This book is the result of just some of the best things that we have learned during our first 20 years on air. Parts of it were first published a few years back as *The Friendly Guide to Music*, but this brand new edition has been considerably expanded to provide you with a far fuller guide to immersing yourself in all aspects of the world of classical music.

So, if you are standing in a bookshop reading this, wondering whether to buy a copy of this book, then please allow us to help you decide.

If you flick through the next 200 or so pages, you will quickly discover that there are a lot of things that this book is not. It is not the most detailed and learned book about classical music that you will be able to lay your hands on in any high street bookshop. It is not packed full of impenetrable musicological arguments about contrapuntal syncopation, or microscopic analysis of a long-forgotten composer's unpublished work. In short, it is not going to be much help to you if you are already an expert in the subject, busily researching your PhD thesis.

Instead, this is the book about classical music for everyone else – and especially for people who wouldn't normally consider buying a book on the subject, but who are, nonetheless, interested in developing a greater understanding of classical music.

If that sounds like you, then you will be pleased to hear that, just like Classic FM itself, this book is mercifully free of the jargon that is sometimes associated with the classical music world. At the same time, we will try to explain some of the terms that those in the know tend to use when they're talking about classical music, so that you can confidently join in with conversations. We've also found that a working knowledge of the terminology can be helpful in getting a little bit more out of listening to the tunes.

The advent of pop music meant that, for a significant part of the 20th century, classical music came to be regarded as the preserve of a cultural elite. Those people inside the classical club didn't seem to want to share the musical delights that they had discovered with those people who were outside the elite. For people looking in, classical music seemed to be surrounded by an impenetrable ring of steel.

The Three Tenors' concert in Rome during the World Cup finals of 1990 marked a resurgence in popular interest in classical music.

The belief that classical music can be enjoyed by everybody, no matter what their age, class or geographical location, is one of the cornerstones on which Classic FM was founded in 1992. It is an ideal to which we have remained absolutely true in the two decades since.

It is worth remembering that classical music was in fact the popular music of its day. In the days before radio, television, the internet and any recordings, what we now consider to be classical music was played in churches, palaces, coffee houses, concert halls and ordinary homes across Europe. The composers who created it were writing music that would be performed at specific occasions and enjoyed by audiences or congregations far and wide. Music and the arts were regarded as having a civilising effect on society, whether the particular works were religious or secular in their nature.

SO WHAT EXACTLY IS CLASSICAL MUSIC?

This is one of the questions that is most often asked of us at Classic FM. And we thought it was something that we ought to tackle up front, before we really get going.

The strictest definition of classical music is everything that was written in the Classical period (between 1750 and 1830), but today we understand classical music to be much more than music composed in just those 80 years.

Calling a piece of music 'classical' is sometimes done as a means of generically distinguishing it from 'popular' music. One of the major tests of whether a tune is or isn't classical music has traditionally been whether it has a sense of 'permanence' about it, in that it is still being performed many years after its composition. This argument begins to fall down as the heritage of pop music becomes ever longer, with hits from the 1950s still being played on the radio today, well over half a century after their original release. It is also hard for us to tell whether a newly written piece of classical music will indeed attain that level of 'permanence' in the future.

The *Concise Oxford Dictionary of Music* offers the following as one of its definitions of classical music:

Music of an orderly nature, with qualities of clarity and balance, and emphasising formal beauty rather than emotional expression (which is not to say that emotion is lacking).

It is true to say that much of classical music follows specific rules of style and form, which we will discuss further in Chapters 4 to 9. However, this definition is still not quite a catch-all.

One of the most striking differences between classical and pop music is the different way the two genres place their emphasis on the relative importance of the composer and the performer. In pop music the performer is all, but in classical music the composer is the star of the show. It is his or her name that tends to come first in the credits and it is he or she who is remembered by history. Take Mozart's *Clarinet Concerto* as an example. Not many people remember Anton Stadler, the clarinettist for whom it was written, but everyone knows Mozart's name. Conversely, if you ask most music fans whom they would most associate with that hardy perennial '*White Christmas*'; they would reply 'Bing Crosby', rather than the song's composer, Irving Berlin.

Some of those self-appointed members of classical music's ruling elite like to claim that film scores sit outside the world of classical music. Yet the first dedicated soundtrack was composed by Camille Saint-Saëns for the 1908 film *L'Assassinat du Duc de Guise*. Since then, Copland, Vaughan Williams, Walton, Prokofiev and Shostakovich have all written music for the cinema. If we go back to the time of Beethoven, we find him composing incidental music for the theatre of the day. Had cinema been invented in his lifetime, he would undoubtedly have written this genre of music too. Throughout classical music's history, composers have always written music for those who pay, whether their patrons were rich noblemen or rich film studios.

Today, film soundtracks are among the most popular symphonic works being composed, with pieces by the likes of John Williams, Hans Zimmer, Howard Shore and James Horner providing an excellent gateway into wider listening to classical music.

Whatever the definition of classical music to which you personally subscribe, we think that the great jazz trumpeter Louis Armstrong had things just about right, when he said: 'There's only two ways to sum up music: either it's good or it's bad. If it's good you don't mess about it – you just enjoy it.'

We hope that you enjoy uncovering the rich tapestry of sounds, emotions and stories that go together to make up classical music. And we hope that you will come to share our view that this is truly the greatest music ever written.

Darren Henley
Sam Jackson
April 2012

HOW TO USE THIS BOOK

This is a book of three thirds. The first part of the book is a guide to immersing yourself in the world of classical music, with everything you ever wanted to know (but were too afraid to ask) about all sorts of subjects, including instruments, orchestras, musical terms, going to classical concerts and creating your own classical music collection.

The next six chapters of the book take you on a journey through the five main eras of classical music: Early, Baroque, Classical, Romantic and the 20th and 21st centuries. You will find handy 'At a glance' guides to each of the main composers featured in the book in the boxes throughout these six chapters.

This is intended to give you an overview of classical music's development from its earliest times right through to the present day. There is so much classical music that has been composed over the years that it would be impossible to include all of it in this one slim volume. Instead, we have concentrated here on the main composers and pieces of music that you will hear played regularly on Classic FM. We have added in one or two other composers whose music we play less often but who have had an important role in the development of classical music.

Towards the back of the book, we have put together a reference section, packed full of classical music statistics and facts, which you might want to draw on to drop into the odd conversation, as the need arises. We have also included a guide to who was composing what when, so that you can see how composers' lives overlapped.

We wanted to make this book as easy on the eye as possible, so we have adopted the following rules throughout:

- Titles of all musical works are set in italics.

- Songs and arias appear in italics within quotation marks.

- Nicknames for a particular work also appear in italics within quotation marks, usually after the work's formal title.

- By and large, we have avoided using opus numbers; however there are some occasions where a composer wrote more than one piece with the same title – and here we have included the opus number, to make it clear which work we are talking about.

- One or two composers have catalogue numbering systems – so if, for instance, you come across the occasional 'K' number (which stands for Ludwig von Köchel, who compiled the catalogue of Mozart's music) or 'D' number (for Otto Deutsch, who did the same for Schubert), you should just treat these the same as you would an opus number. We've put them in only where needed, in order to identify a particular piece.

It was the turn of the 21st century, somewhere in a relatively soulless office building in Manchester. A group of Classic FM listeners was sitting drinking coffee, while a few of us observed their discussions through one of those glass panes that lets you see only one way. We wanted to gain an insight into listeners' lives, to find out why they enjoyed classical music, and to see what we could do to give people like them an even better radio station. People just like the man in his early thirties who spoke with passion about how classical music calmed him down when he was driving.

'The thing is, though,' he commented, 'before I turn the engine off when I get home, I always flick over to a pop music station.'

'Why is that?' the person facilitating the discussion asked.

'Because if my girlfriend ever got in the car and I turned on the engine, I couldn't bear her to know that I sometimes listen to classical music.'

This book is for people like that man and, we hope, for people like you. We're passionate about classical music, and over the last 20 years Classic FM's very existence has been predicated on the idea that this wonderfully rich, exciting, emotional music can and should be available to absolutely everyone. But that's not to say it comes without its baggage. Many people wrongly assume that classical music could never be for them, whereas we believe that no one should live without experiencing it. And let's be absolutely clear: loving classical music is something to shout from the rooftops, rather than to be shy about. In fact, you would probably be surprised just how many people from all walks of life we have met over the years who have discovered classical music and now share our passion for listening to it.

During the first section of this book, we'll be uncovering exactly what classical music is all about and how to make sense of the seemingly insurmountable jargon. Why on earth should we care if something is 'in F sharp minor' – and what does it mean, anyway? What's the difference between a concerto and a cadenza, or a symphony and a sonata? And if you're looking to start a classical music collection, should you play it safe with a compilation, venture into some complex and challenging contemporary music, or purchase nothing but Mozart symphonies for the next 40 years? (The answer, by the way, is none of the above – but we'll come to that a little later.)

One of the biggest obstacles for people approaching classical music is the presumption that they probably need to have spent years studying Musical Analysis, along with fluency in multiple European languages, before embarking on any enjoyment of the tunes themselves. When you come to Classic FM for the first time, only to discover that you're hearing the *'Españoleta y Fanfare de la Caballería de Nápoles'* from Rodrigo's *Fantasia Para un Gentilhombre* performed by José María Gallardo del Rey and the Spanish National Orchestra conducted by Rafael Frühbeck de Burgos, your first concern may well be the need to draw breath rather than anything related to the music. But once you start to grasp the classical lingo, everything begins to make a lot more sense. What's more, it's by no means necessary to be able to converse in Italian before you can happily sit through a Puccini opera and be unexpectedly moved to tears.

Over the next few pages, we'll take a whistle-stop tour through some of the most common musical terms, flagging up what they mean and pointing you in the direction of some composers who show them off in a brilliant way. By the end of this first section, you'll undoubtedly know your 'presto' from your 'pizzicato' and your 'forte' from your 'fugue'. Along the way, we'll pick out some of the moments in history that link in with classical music, showing how Impressionism didn't reach only as far as the visual arts, for example. There'll be a quick nod towards different genres, answering those niggling little questions such as: what's the 'chamber' in 'chamber music' all about? And we'll uncover who the composers were, why they're important, and how you should go about beginning to encounter some of their finest music.

Getting into classical music partly involves understanding what it all means – but that's fairly pointless unless you actually take the chance to experience it, which is where the next section comes in. With a few notable exceptions, you can be pretty sure that, wherever you are in the UK, you're within a ten-mile radius of a decent concert taking place this month. Admittedly, not every one of them will be a full symphony orchestra (it's been a while since the Philharmonia toured to Land's End) but we're a country that's blessed with a huge amount of excellent professional and amateur music-making. Every week, concert halls, churches and community spaces host an impressive variety of events – and, in recent years, all sorts of more unconventional venues have become places to encounter classical music. Puccini in the pub is a reality in north London, for example, and you can now experience the Bach *Passions* performed in a city warehouse.

As you'll discover over the coming pages, there are all sorts of handy ways to work out exactly which concerts are worth your time and money, and what route you should take if you want to experience a particular style of music. Also crucially important, though, is the whole etiquette of concert-going. Many people are put off from turning up to a classical concert for fear that they'll have to dress like an extra in *Downton Abbey* before they're even allowed into the building. And once you get past the box office, what exactly should you do? Is it OK to clap? Can you chat in between movements? And what on earth should you wear?

All these questions, and more, will be tackled as part of our guide to getting into classical music.

CHAPTER 1

UNRAVELLING THE JARGON

Local music shops are fairly predictable places. Inside pretty much every one you'll find a selection of beautiful instruments, a man who's been there for about 30 years who knows an unbelievable amount about clarinet reeds, and a selection of tea towels containing all sorts of brilliantly dreadful musical puns. 'Rubato' is 'ointment for a musician's back'; 'Quaver' is 'the feeling before a lesson when you haven't practised'; 'Syncopation' is 'a bowel condition brought on by an overdose of jazz'.

Classical music is awash with jargon, which probably explains the success of these rather naff tea towels, but is any of it actually useful? After all, Johann Sebastian Bach, no less, once described music as being 'nothing remarkable', saying, 'All one has to do is hit the right keys at the right time and the instrument plays itself.'

However, in the same way that understanding the offside rule assists you in following what's going on in a football match, so knowing a few technical terms can help you navigate your way through your favourite classical music. Over the next few pages, we've picked out some of the most common ones, giving you a potted guide to exactly what they mean and why they're important. Understanding these terms will mean that you begin to hear your favourite music in a new way, as the jargon transforms into your very own musical vocabulary.

♫ A cappella

Allegri's *Miserere* is one of the most famous and most haunting pieces in all of classical music. Tallis's *Spem in Alium* similarly sends shivers down your spine, as does the choral arrangement of Barber's *Adagio for Strings*. And they're all united by one thing: the choir isn't accompanied by any instruments. When you hear the sound of voices alone, you can be sure that what you're listening to is being performed a cappella.

♫ Accelerando

A fairly easy one, this: the musical equivalent of shouting, 'Get a move on!' Decellerando, by contrast, tells the musician to slow down and take everything at a much more leisurely pace.

♫ Adagio

The term 'adagio' literally means 'at ease'. Musically, it's an indication to play the piece slowly – as you'll hear in works such as Albinoni's *Adagio in G minor*, Khachaturian's *Adagio of Spartacus and Phrygia* (the *Onedin Line* theme tune) or the '*Rose Adagio*' from Tchaikovsky's *The Sleeping Beauty*. If you're wondering exactly how slowly something should be played when it's marked 'adagio', consider that there are 60 seconds in a minute, and if something is at 'adagio' pace it should move along at around the 70 beats per minute mark.

♫ Allegro

The exact opposite of adagio, allegro is an instruction to play quickly. You're looking at cramming about 150 beats per minute into anything with 'allegro' written at the top of the manuscript paper. A good musical example of this can be heard a few minutes into Elgar's beautiful *Introduction and Allegro for Strings*.

♫ Alto

In the world of singing, the alto rarely gets the glory. In nearly every opera, the soprano or the mezzo-soprano (both of whom we'll come to a little later) is given the star role, while the lowly alto is all too often relegated to a bit part. The term 'alto' can refer to a woman whose vocal range is relatively low, but it can also be applied to instruments. An alto saxophone, for example, is the most famous instrument from that family (the soprano sax looks a little like a golden clarinet and has a high pitch, whereas a baritone saxophone is bigger and deeper than the alto).

♫ Andante

Another speed-related Italian musical term; the literal definition of 'andante' is 'at a walking pace'. Which invites the question, 'How fast should I walk?' The slightly vague answer to that one is: 'Faster than you would if you were listening to an adagio, but not so fast that you're running at allegro.' The most fitting musical example of an andante is the second movement of Tchaikovsky's *String Quartet No.1*, most often heard nowadays in an arrangement for cello and string quartet and dubbed the *'Andante cantabile'* (which translates as 'at a walking pace, and played in a song-like manner').

♫ Aria

Although nowadays almost exclusively applied to opera, the word 'aria' dates all the way back to the 14th century. It's the Italian word for 'air', and was applied originally to a particularly graceful melody; today, though, it almost exclusively describes an operatic song performed by one singer plus orchestra. To confuse matters slightly, an aria can also be an instrumental piece (the aria from Bach's *Goldberg Variations* for solo keyboard, for example) or a vocal work that wasn't written originally for the stage – in which case, it's a concert aria. Mozart wrote a fair few of these, as did Beethoven. Some of the most famous arias in the world of opera include Puccini's *'O Mio Babbino Caro'* from the opera *Gianni Schicchi* and Mozart's *'Queen of the Night Aria'* from *The Magic Flute*, both of which are performed by a soprano, as well as the tenor favourites *'La Donna è Mobile'* from Verdi's *Rigoletto* and *'Che Gelida Manina'* from Puccini's *La Bohème*.

♫ Baritone

This is another one of those terms that pertains to the range of notes a singer or instrument is capable of. Baritone sits somewhere in between a bass and a tenor; in Mozart's opera *Don Giovanni*, the title role is sung by a baritone, so that's a good one to go along to if you want to hear this kind of voice in action. Famous baritones today include Dmitri Hvorostovsky, Thomas Hampson and Simon Keenlyside, while Bryn Terfel describes himself as a bass-baritone.

♫ Bass

The lowest of the low, from the bass clarinet (a fabulous instrument that was put to good use in orchestras from the late 19th century onwards) through to bass singers such as the much loved Sir John Tomlinson.

♫ Cadenza

A cadenza is basically a great chance for a soloist to show off. You'll often find one occurring in a concerto: the orchestra will have been accompanying the soloist from the word go, until the soloist suddenly appears to break free and play unaccompanied, demonstrating the capabilities of the instrument and sheer personal ability to play an awful lot of notes in a short space of time. Some cadenzas are put in by the composer; others are written by the soloist.

♫ Chamber Music

Duets, trios, quartets, quintets: all could be described as chamber music. The term we use today originates from the days of Haydn and Mozart, when music was written to be performed by a small group of players in a relatively small room. The difference between chamber music and orchestral music is that there's only ever one player per part – whereas in an orchestra, there could be a whole host of string players performing the first violin part alone. Just over a hundred years ago, chamber music was described by one scholar as 'music with friends', which is probably the most apt description of all.

♫ Clef

You know that squiggle you see at the start of a piece of music – the one that looks slightly like an ampersand that has had a bit of cosmetic surgery? Well, that's a clef – the treble clef, to be precise.

'Clef' is the French word for 'key'. The particular symbol that is used at the start of the music dictates exactly what pitch the notes are on the lines that follow. So, if a composer's writing a melody for, say, a piano or a flute, they'll probably use the treble clef. And if they're writing for lower instruments, they'll employ the bass clef. There are also one or two less common clefs that cater for instruments whose range falls between the treble and bass clefs.

♫ Coda
Another Italian term, which literally translates as 'tail'. And that gives you some idea of where it might fit within a piece of music: unsurprisingly, the coda comes at the end. Composers often include a coda to ensure that their music finishes with a real flourish. Mozart was a fan of this approach with his piano sonatas – have a listen to *No. 11*, with its well-known *'Rondo alla Turca'* at the end, for ample proof of this.

♫ Concerto
Nowadays, the term 'concerto' refers to a piece of music composed for solo instrument plus orchestra. Its origin, though, was back in Baroque times, and the concerto grosso form. This involved grouping together a bunch of musicians as a sort of ensemble of soloists to perform alongside the larger orchestra. From the mid-18th century onwards, the concerto grosso fell out of fashion – but the idea of composing orchestral music that included a solo instrumentalist became ever more popular. There are hundreds of brilliant musical examples of this: try Elgar's *Cello Concerto* for starters, followed by Rachmaninov's *Piano Concerto No. 2*, Mozart's *Clarinet Concerto*, Mendelssohn's *Violin Concerto* and, for something a little more off the beaten track, Glière's astonishing *Harp Concerto*.

♫ Consonance and Dissonance
Most musical terms can be traced to Italy in one way or another; these two derive from Latin words – one of which, 'sonare', means 'to sound'. The 'con' of consonance means 'with', whereas the 'dis' of dissonance is most closely translated as 'without' or 'apart'.

Consonance, then, refers to music that sounds tuneful and harmonious; dissonance relates to music that is much less easy on the ear. As we shall discover later, in the 20th century, a whole bunch of composers from the Second Viennese School (Schoenberg and Webern, for example) revelled in dissonance, turning their backs on traditional melody and going out of their way to write works that are much more challenging to the average listener. The vast majority of classical music is consonant, though.

♫ Ensemble

There are two distinct meanings to this one. The first relates to a group of musicians. An orchestra is an ensemble; so is a small group of players; so is a choir. Quite simply, it's a crowd of people who have got together to play music. The other definition is all about how well the musicians are playing. If you hear someone remark that there was 'great ensemble' in the performance, it's praise for how well the musicians were playing together, and how united they were in their precision and sound.

♫ Espressivo

Although you might be tempted to think you could order a double one of these at the local coffee shop, 'espressivo' is actually the Italian translation of the English word 'expressive'. So, if it's marked at the top of a piece of music, the player knows he or she should perform it in a particularly heart-on-your-sleeve sort of way.

♫ Etude

The French word 'étude' means 'study' – and, in music, an étude is a composition designed to improve a particular element of the player's technique. They are most commonly piano pieces; Chopin's set of *Etudes* is an excellent example.

♫ Falsetto

For many men, the word 'falsetto' takes them back to their early teenage years, and those excruciatingly embarrassing moments when their voice would fluctuate from a Barry White bass to a Bee Gees squeal. Falsetto refers to the vocal range that men are able to employ by relaxing their vocal chords, and singing approximately one octave (so, eight notes) above their usual pitch. Think *'Staying Alive'*, but in classical music. Counter-tenors such as Andreas Scholl sing permanently within the falsetto range.

♫ Flat and Sharp

If you are new to classical music, the use of the terms 'flat' and 'sharp' can be quite baffling. You'll often come across phrases such as 'in D flat major' or 'in F sharp minor' as part of the title of a work. The good news is that the meaning of 'flat' and 'sharp' are pretty simple: a D flat is slightly lower than a D (on a piano keyboard, it's the black note to the left), whereas a D sharp is slightly higher (the black note to the right). If you hear someone describe a singer as being 'a bit sharp' or 'a bit flat', chances are they're singing out of tune, a little above or below the right note, and could have done with warming up with some vocal exercises first before opening their mouth. If something is described as being 'in D flat major', then the central note of the piece of music – the note that feels like 'home' – is D flat; 'D flat major' is the key signature – more of which later (along with major and minor).

♫ Forte

The Italian for 'loud', 'forte' (pronounced 'for-tay') is a term that relates to the dynamics, or volume, of the piece in question. Its bigger brother, fortissimo, means 'really loud'; in Ravel's love-it-or-hate-it *Boléro*, the volume begins at *ppp* (an über-quiet version of piano, the opposite of forte), and ends at *fff*.

♫ Fugue

Bach's *Toccata and Fugue in D minor* is one of the most famous pieces in all classical music – and it's probably the best-known organ work in the world. We'll tackle what a toccata is in a few pages' time – but what about a fugue? Well, the term is effectively the classical music version of 'call and response': a theme (known as the 'subject') is set up at the start; that theme is then imitated and elaborated on; and, before long, there's a great wash of sound being created by all this overlapping repetition. Bach composed hundreds of fugues, and his set of *48 Preludes and Fugues* for keyboard is an absolute must. There are a fair few examples of fugues from the time of Mozart onwards, the most substantial of which is Shostakovich's *24 Preludes and Fugues*.

♫ Glissando

Incredibly satisfying for any pianist, not least because it's very easy to do, a glissando is the technique of running your fingers down the keyboard very quickly from top to bottom or from bottom to top. A glissando can be performed on other instruments, too – the harp, for example – but it's heard most often on the piano. In popular music, a glissando is famously used in the Boomtown Rats' single *'I Don't Like Mondays'*; in classical music, there are all sorts of notable examples. If you have a few moments to spare, take a look at Alex Ross's blog on the *New Yorker* website (www.newyorker.com): his article 'The Top Ten Glissandos' includes audio clips of everything from Stravinsky's *The Rite of Spring* to Gershwin's *Rhapsody in Blue*, via Led Zeppelin's *'Whole Lotta Love'* and Nina Simone singing *'Strange Fruit'*.

♫ Grandioso

A fairly easy-to-guess one, this: 'grandioso' means 'to play grandly'. It's often used in music from the Romantic era: the orchestral works of Wagner, for example.

♫ Grave

Pronounced to rhyme with 'halve', this means the slowest of the slow. The only musical term that could conceivably suggest playing a piece of music more slowly and solemnly than grave is larghetto.

♫ Grazioso

Another descriptive Italian term, this one instructs the musician to play gracefully. It's often used in music from the Classical period – so, Mozart, Boccherini, Haydn and the like.

♫ Homophony

The prefix 'homo' at the start of a word comes from the Greek, meaning 'the same'. And in the case of homophony, it's all about the way in which different lines of music are played together. Effectively, anything that's performed in a chord-like structure, with all the parts moving together, is an example of homophony, while lines that go off in all sorts of different, intricate directions create polyphony. Most hymn tunes are clear examples of homophony in action.

♫ Impressionism

The visual art of painters such as Monet is often described as being 'Impressionist'. Similarly, the music of early 20th-century French composers such as Debussy or Ravel displays comparable aural characteristics. If you can picture the hazy, dream-like images evoked by the finest Impressionist paintings, imagine a similar kind of music. Then listen to Debussy's *Prélude à l'après midi d'un faune* and you'll hear it taking place before your very ears.

♫ Impromptu

An impromptu gathering of friends is something delightfully spur of the moment, unplanned and enjoyable. In music, an impromptu is exactly the same: a piece that is meant to sound off the cuff, fun, almost flippant – as if the composer had dashed it off at the piano before skipping out the door. Schubert's famous *Impromptus* demonstrate this amply, as does the ever popular *Fantaisie-Impromptu in C sharp minor* by Chopin.

♫ Intermezzo

An intermezzo is a sort of musical version of an intermission: something that happens in between the action, most often within an opera. One act has finished, the next one is about to begin, but in between, there's a scene change. So what does the composer do to fill the time? Answer: compose an instrumental intermezzo. The most famous intermezzo in classical music is the divine three-minute orchestral miniature from Mascagni's opera *Cavalleria Rusticana*. Some composers have also written stand-alone intermezzos (or, to be grammatically correct if we're using Italian, 'intermezzi') – for example Brahms, whose *Intermezzi, Opus 117* for piano are three of the most beautiful, heartbreaking creations in the history of classical music.

♫ Interval

In music, an interval relates to the gap between two particular notes. If you play middle C on the piano, consider that to be note number one. Move up to note number three (so, past D and on to E) and you're playing an interval of a third. A major chord involves playing the original note (the 'tonic') plus the third and the fifth; in this case, C, E and G.

♫ Intonation

This one links in with the idea of musical sharps and flats. Many a cry of 'Watch your intonation!' has gone out across a school orchestra. If the player is a little off key, the intonation is out. It's all about how closely the musician has managed to play the note in relation to its pure, absolute pitch.

♫ Key Signature

Here's another term that's associated with sharps and flats. Basically, the whole sound-world of pretty much every piece of Western classical music centres in on one major or minor chord. The central note – the one that most phrases or passages return to in the end – is the same note as the key signature. The key signature could be anything from C major to B flat minor; to hear a good musical example, try listening to Bach's *Well-Tempered Clavier*, a set of 48 preludes and fugues on the piano or harpsichord in every single key signature.

♫ Legato

Meaning 'smoothly', legato is the opposite of staccato – which we'll come to later. To hear a great example of legato in action, try the heavenly third movement of Rachmaninov's *Symphony No. 2*, with its wonderfully sweeping strings.

♫ Leitmotif

In many pieces of music, but particularly in opera, one particular phrase or set of notes is used to herald the arrival or fate of a particular character – and that set of notes is what is meant by the term 'leitmotif'. Without wanting to trivialise some of the greatest pieces of music ever written, the concept of leitmotif is not a million miles away from the booing and hissing that occurs every time a pantomime villain appears on stage. Wagner used the idea of leitmotif most extensively, but you can also hear a version of it put to good use by Berlioz in his *Symphonie Fantastique*, which features a recurring theme depicting the woman the composer was infatuated with.

♫ Libretto

Every great song needs a great lyricist – and, in classical music, the writer of the words is known as the librettist. The libretto is the text a composer sets to music, whether in the operas of Puccini or the light-hearted comedies of Gilbert and Sullivan.

♫ Major and Minor

As we've already mentioned, 'major' and 'minor' relate to a piece of music's key signature. At its most basic level, music in a major key sounds happy; music in a minor key sounds sad. Every single note on the piano keyboard has a major and minor key signature – so we get E major and E minor, F major and F minor, and so on.

♫ Mezzo

The Italian for 'middle' or 'medium', 'mezzo' can relate to issues of volume ('mezzo-forte', for example, translates as 'quite loud') or to singers: a mezzo-soprano is a woman who has a fairly high voice but whose range is pitched lower than that of a soprano.

♫ Minuet

This courtly dance was put to its most famous use by the Italian composer Luigi Boccherini, whose *'Minuet'* from the *String Quintet in E* received unexpected fame through its inclusion in the film *The*

Ladykillers. Originally a dance, the minuet was then regularly employed in the form of a minuet and trio by all sorts of Classical-era composers – most often in the third movement of their symphonies.

♫ Modulation

This is the classical music equivalent of the moment when, in pop music, all four members of a boyband get up off their stools and walk forward in a cloud of dry ice as the music shifts up a notch. This change in key signature or musical centre is known as a modulation; it's regularly used in sonatas when the second 'subject' or theme is introduced, but is also employed in pretty much every other kind of music around.

♫ Motif

We've already covered leitmotif – so you've probably already worked out that a motif is a short musical phrase that recurs at various points within a piece of music. Sometimes, it's nothing more than a jolly little set of notes that acts as a unifying sound across the course of the work; at other times, though, a motif can be altogether more sinister: take, for example, the 'fate' motif heard in Tchaikovsky's *Symphony No. 5*.

♫ Movement

Many pieces of classical music are separated into individually numbered movements, which nearly always have a short pause in proceedings between them. The most famous exception to this rule is between the second and third movements of Beethoven's *Piano Concerto No. 5 ('Emperor')*; another good exception comes between all three movements of the Mendelssohn *Violin Concerto*. In both cases, there's no gap whatsoever and the movements run together without a moment's hesitation.

♫ Nocturne

Although the Franco-Polish composer Frédéric Chopin is most closely associated with the nocturne (mainly because he wrote so many of them), this form of piano miniature was actually invented by an Irishman called John Field. A nocturne is intended to evoke images of night time, and is often characterised by a dream-like melody played in the right hand, over a simple, repeated pattern in the left hand. Gabriel Fauré also wrote some beautiful piano nocturnes, while the likes of Debussy and Mendelssohn composed orchestral ones, the most famous being the latter's 'Nocturne' from the incidental music for *A Midsummer Night's Dream*.

♫ Opera

Say the word 'opera' to many people who are new to classical music, and what appears is a mental image of a warbling, incredibly overweight woman belting out a tune in a dress that looks as if it took her three hours to put on. Other preconceptions about opera include a fear that it's completely impenetrable, a concern that it lasts for hours on end, and a presumption that you won't have a clue what's going on unless you're a native Italian speaker. Thankfully, opera is far more accessible than any of those misguided stereotypes would suggest. The term relates to a piece of music with an accompanying libretto (see above), which is performed on the stage. Often, operas also have ridiculous plots involving murder (frequently multiple ones), marriage (ditto), extensive cross-dressing and a rather dramatic, unnecessary yet entirely predictable suicide on the part of the heroine just before the final curtain falls. Some of classical music's best and most famous tunes can be found in opera: from Puccini's 'Nessun Dorma' to Verdi's 'Grand March', via Mozart's overture to *The Marriage of Figaro*, and Bizet's *Carmen*.

♫ Operetta

Operetta is opera's mischievous younger cousin. While opera concerns itself with weighty issues of life and death, operetta is all about ridicule, farce and some rollickingly good tunes. England's finest operetta partnership was between W. S. Gilbert and Arthur Sullivan (they of *'I am the very model of a modern major general'* fame). Gilbert penned the libretto and Sullivan the music and, between them, they dominated the genre of operetta in Victorian England.

Other European composers also got in on the act, though – among them, Léhar with *The Merry Widow* and Offenbach with *La Belle Hélène*. The genre crossed the pond, too, and was best exhibited in America by Bernstein's *Candide*.

♫ Opus

This is one of those words that can be added to the list of 'what's that all about?' terms at the end of a piece of music. A piece of music's opus number is basically its library reference code: the first work a composer wrote is usually his Opus 1 (often abbreviated to Op. 1), and the numbers then continue until we reach the final piece he composed. It's not always that simple, though: the opus number doesn't necessarily relate to the order in which pieces were written but, more accurately, to the order in which they were published. It's neither the most important musical term, nor the most interesting, but it still deserves a mention.

♫ Oratorio

In its most basic form, an oratorio is an opera without the acting. Performances of oratorios take place in the concert hall rather than the theatre – and although you still get the orchestra, the soloists, the choir and the libretto, you don't get the costumes, the movement or the sumptuous sets and lighting. Often biblical or religious in theme, some of the best-known oratorios include Haydn's *The Creation*, Mendelssohn's *Elijah* and Elgar's *The Dream of Gerontius*.

♫ Overture

In opera, the overture is the curtain-raiser to the action, often containing some of the most significant musical motifs, which we're about to hear as the plot unfolds. Performed by the musicians alone, with the singers nearly always having yet to appear, overtures are often incredibly popular pieces of music in their own right (Mozart's overtures to *The Magic Flute* and *The Marriage of Figaro*, for example). From the early 1800s onwards, composers begin to write stand-alone overtures – none more so than Beethoven, whose *Coriolan Overture* and three *Leonore Overtures* are perennially popular on the concert hall platform today. And who could forget Mendelssohn's stormy *Hebrides Overture*, inspired by the composer's trip to the Scottish island of Staffa, or Tchaikovsky's magnificent *1812 Overture*, written to celebrate a Russian military victory over France?

♫ Partita

This term is used almost exclusively in Baroque music – and, within Baroque music, almost exclusively by Johann Sebastian Bach. He used the word as an alternative to 'suite', indicating a collection of movements, often in dance rhythms. Today, his violin partitas are the best-known example of the word in musical action.

♫ Piano

We realise what you might be thinking: 'I know what a piano looks and sounds like.' But how about when it's pronounced 'pee-AAAAH-no'? It's one little change, but it makes a big difference: in this context, 'piano' is the Italian word for 'soft', meaning quietly. The opposite of forte, piano instructs the musician to play at a low volume; if preceded by the Italian term 'mezzo', the music should be played 'fairly softly'.

♫ Pizzicato

A vital technique for anyone who plays a stringed instrument, pizzicato describes what happens when, rather than using a bow, the performer downs tools and plucks the strings with his or her fingers instead. Great examples include Johann Strauss Jnr's *Pizzicato Polka* and Britten's *'Playful Pizzicato'* from his *A Simple Symphony*.

♫ Polyphony

The opposite of homophony, polyphony is a description of musical lines going in all sorts of different (yet entirely complementary) directions within a single piece of music. If homophony is all about hymn-like chords, polyphony is a glorious wall of sound, with interweaving threads of music fitting together like a perfect patchwork quilt. Possibly the finest ever example is Thomas Tallis's

Spem in Alium: 40 separate voices, each singing a different part, united in creating one of the most glorious pieces in the history of classical music.

♫ Presto
Another Italian term relating to speed – and no prizes for guessing that this one requires the musician to play quickly!

♫ Rallentando and Ritardando
These two similar Italian terms both act as the polar opposite of accelerando. In other words, if you see them written on a piece of music, you know you need to slow down gradually to a complete standstill.

♫ Recitative
If the arias in an opera are where you'll find the best melodies, the recitative sections are altogether less heartbreaking. The term describes what happens when the composer wants to get a large section of the plot away in one go: gone are the lyrical musical lines; in their place are quickly sung and rather matter-of-fact pieces of information, which serve the job of letting us know what's happening plot-wise, but do little to remain in the memory music-wise.

♫ Requiem
From Mozart and Fauré to Britten and Verdi, some of the greatest of the great composers have written a requiem – and, what's more, they have placed some of their most glorious melodies within them. A requiem is a Mass for the Dead, often setting a particular Catholic text. Not all requiems follow this format, though: the contemporary composer and Classic FM presenter Howard Goodall, for example, wrote a requiem specifically for those who grieve, rather than being solely in memory of those who have passed away.

♫ Rococo

You might already know this term from its use in the visual arts or literature, and its musical definition is exactly the same as in any of these forms. 'Rococo' describes a post-Baroque time in history in which artists of all kinds reacted against the restrictive rules of the period. In music, this meant abandoning some of the strict definitions of musical structure, and opting instead for elegance and intricacy. The French composer Rameau wrote all sorts of ornate rococo music; another good example is Tchaikovsky's *Variations on a Rococo Theme* for cello and orchestra.

♫ Rondo

Remember Kenny Ball and his Jazzmen, with their 1963 hit *Rondo*? No, us neither. But if you give it a listen, you'll hear that it was based on Mozart's *'Rondo alla Turca'* from the composer's *Piano Sonata No. 11*. A theme appears, something else happens, then back comes the theme, then we're off elsewhere, and then ... Look! It's that theme again! There, in a nutshell, is your definition of the term 'rondo'. The use of a main theme that continues to return throughout the piece of music has been used by all sorts of composers for centuries.

♫ Rubato

Music from the Romantic era has a particularly special aural quality: it seems to ebb and flow beautifully, to tug on the heart strings, almost to breathe and sigh. The reason? More often than not, it's because of the use of 'rubato' – an Italian term that literally means 'stolen time'. Rather than rigidly following a very strict beat, the music is pulled and pushed, stretched and squashed, into something that sounds less mechanical and, many would say, more human. Sometimes, composers specify its use; at other times, the performer takes a healthy helping of artistic licence. But either way, when it works, the effect is mesmerising.

♫ Scherzo

You'll often hear the word 'scherzo' within the phrase 'the scherzo from ...' Frequently, a scherzo is another term for the third movement of a symphony or sonata. At other times, it describes a particular kind of music, quite light and even jokey in style. That's certainly the case with the *'Scherzo'* from Mendelssohn's incidental music for *A Midsummer Night's Dream*; it's worth pointing out that, in Italian, the word 'scherzo' literally translates as 'joke'.

♫ Sonata

This term has evolved in all sorts of ways over time but, more often that not, it describes a piece of music for solo keyboard, or solo instrument plus keyboard accompaniment. Often in three separate movements – a fast one, a slow one, and another fast one to finish – the sonata became hugely popular during the Classical period, when composers such as Mozart and Haydn wrote them by the dozen. Beethoven composed the most famous piano sonata of them all: his *Piano Sonata No. 14 in C sharp minor*, better known by its nickname, the *'Moonlight Sonata'*. It's one of the few sonatas that bucks the fast–slow–fast trend, beginning with a famously hypnotic opening movement.

♫ Soprano

This is another term that relates to an instrument's range – and by 'instrument', we most definitely include the voice here. Many of the world's most famous singers were sopranos, from legends such as Maria Callas and Joan Sutherland to the modern-day stars Cecilia Bartoli and Anna Netrebko. It's the highest range an instrument is capable of, and if you fancy discovering a truly amazing soprano, have a listen to the soprano saxophone!

♫ Staccato

'Staccato' is an Italian word that translates as 'detached' – but not in the 'I'm really not very interested' sense of the word. Instead, it means the player should play each of the notes in a short and separate way, rather than as one lyrical line. In this respect, it's the exact opposite of legato. A good example of staccato in action is the stately opening to Elgar's *Pomp and Circumstance March No. 4*.

♩ Symphony

Here's another term that's evolved over time, but that today nearly always refers to a piece of orchestral music composed from the 18th century onwards. Almost without exception, a symphony will have three or four movements, with many following the same template: an upbeat opening movement followed by an adagio, a scherzo and a lively finale. Mozart composed 41 symphonies, Haydn 104, and Beethoven only nine. Still, fans of the German master will happily argue that it's a case of quality over quantity.

♩ Tempo

A simple one, this: the word 'tempo' is Italian for 'time', and therefore relates to the speed a piece is played.

♩ Tenor

If all the best female roles in opera go to the soprano, their male equivalent is nearly always the tenor. The three most famous tenors of all time were, aptly enough, 'The Three Tenors' – Luciano Pavarotti, Placido Domingo and José Carreras – who wowed the world with their operatic performances in Rome during the Italia 90 football World Cup. Being a musical term related to pitch, the word 'tenor' can also be applied to instruments other than the voice: the tenor horn, for example, is worth a listen, as is the tenor saxophone. Give the tenor banjo a wide berth, though, unless you're of a particularly strong musical disposition.

♩ Time Signature

Have you ever wondered exactly what the conductor is doing when he or she waves his or her arms in front of an orchestra? Well, one of the most important roles is to 'beat time' – in other words, to make sure all the musicians keep playing to the same beat. In music, the time signature is the number of beats in each bar.

♩ Toccata

If you're a keyboard player and you want a sure-fire way of showing off, you can do a lot worse than learn a toccata. This particular type of music, made famous by Bach's *Toccata and Fugue in D minor* for organ, is designed to showcase the abundant skills of the soloist. Another great example is Schumann's *Toccata* for piano, which is fiendishly difficult to play.

♫ Vibrato

Don't get a classical music anorak started on this one. In brief: vibrato is a technique used mainly by singers and string players to create a particularly shimmering musical effect. When using vibrato, the musician will skilfully move pitch ever so slightly, returning to the original pitch almost immediately, and repeat this process over and over within a very short space of time. It's the way in which operatic sopranos achieve that famous 'wobble' in their voices. But the controversy here is that musicians and historians really do get their knickers in a twist about when vibrato should be used. For many years (in fact, for most of the 20th century), all classical music was performed with vibrato. Then, along came the 1970s: a post-Flower Power period when most of the Western world was transfixed with 'make love, not war' but the classical music Establishment was focused on the rights and wrongs of authentic period performance. All of a sudden, vibrato was deemed to be very wrong in certain musical circles, and there was a rush of new recordings without it. You have been warned: bring up vibrato among a bunch of musicologists at your peril.

♫ Virtuoso

A performer who is unbelievably talented and who can dazzle with his or her instrument is often referred to as a 'virtuoso'. It's another Italian term, applied throughout history to composers such as Paganini and Liszt, who were also astonishing players in their own right. Not all composers approve of virtuosos (or, *virtuosi* to use the correct Italian plural), though: Wagner once famously remarked that he disliked their 'triviality and exhibitionist talents'.

♫ Vivace

Another Italian speed-related term, 'vivace' instructs the musician to play quickly. The word literally translates as 'lively' or 'vivid'.

CHAPTER 2

LISTENING TO CLASSICAL MUSIC LIVE

So – you've read the lingo, you know what music you like to listen to, and you're thinking of venturing out to experience a classical music concert live. The question is: what on earth should you go along to? Is a summer pops concert on a well-manicured lawn just as good as the whole of Wagner's *Ring* cycle? Will turning up in jeans and a T-shirt be frowned on – and if so, why? And when on earth is clapping appropriate?

A great many people give live classical music concerts a wide berth because they worry that they won't understand what's happening, or that they won't fit in with those 'in the know'. We absolutely believe that classical music is for everyone, no matter their age, their background, or the state of their jeans, and over the next few pages we'll unpick some of the common questions and concerns about live concerts. With any luck, by the end of the chapter you'll have already signed up to at least one performance taking place in a venue near you.

Before getting into the nitty-gritty of the concert-going experience, the most important thing to be sure of before even setting foot inside the venue is that there's a good chance you'll actually enjoy the music you're about to hear. That sounds like a blindingly obvious point, but unless you know you like the tunes, everything else will pale into insignificance.

First, ask yourself the question: which composers or pieces get your toes tapping? Is there a particular genre of music, be it anything from string quartets to film scores, that lifts your mood and makes you feel proud to be a fan of classical music? And arguably more importantly, what do you definitely *not* like? Too often, it's easy to succumb to a sort of classical music peer pressure: the idea that you couldn't possibly say you don't like Beethoven, or that Mozart's music leaves you cold, for fear of being ostracised by that rather fearsome-looking woman from up the road who sings in a choral society and who looks as if she might eat you alive if you dare to disagree with her musical preferences.

Many people who are starting out on their classical music journey enjoy going along to a concert of very well-known hits. Raymond Gubbay is a visionary concert promoter who has spent more than 40 years putting together highly accessible classical music events in all sorts of places, and his concerts are an excellent place to start. Raymond's 'Classical Spectacular' events at London's Royal Albert Hall, as well as other concert halls and arenas around the country, include fireworks, lights and lasers. Their phenomenal success has led to a broad range of similar events put on by other concert promoters in venues across the UK. If you're a first-time concert-goer, you might well feel that something like this is a good way to dip your toe into live classical music.

On the other hand, it's by no means the case that you need to have formal training and an encyclopedic knowledge of the repertoire to be able to appreciate a standard classical music concert. If the idea of lights, lasers and cannon fills you with dread, there are plenty of other outstanding venues that provide the ideal setting for an initial concert experience.

OUR TEN FAVOURITE CONCERT HALLS

One of the most important questions for any concert-goer concerns where the actual music-making is taking place. Every week, right across the UK, hundreds of public performances are held in traditional halls and theatres, as well as smaller venues, such as churches, schools, even hospitals and pubs. Listed below is our Top Ten of UK concert halls: places where we've experienced fantastic music-making in recent years and where, week after week, there are performances from fine resident ensembles and, very often, visiting orchestras and soloists of equally impressive calibre. Of course, any such list is subjective, and you might well disagree with our choices, but we think they provide a good starting point for anyone looking for a destination that is warm, welcoming and packed full of edge-of-your-seat music-making.

In no particular order, our Top Ten is as follows:

♫ Southbank Centre, London

Located next to Waterloo station on the South Bank of the Thames, this 21-acre site houses some of the UK's best orchestras, and is also regularly packed to bursting with visiting musicians. The Centre, which includes the Royal Festival Hall and the Queen Elizabeth Hall, has an illustrious history stretching back to the 1951 Festival of Britain. As well as the two concert halls, it also houses the Purcell Room, the Hayward Gallery, the Saison Poetry Library and the Arts Council Collection. Resident ensembles include the Philharmonia Orchestra (Classic FM's Orchestra on Tour), the London Philharmonic Orchestra and the Orchestra of the Age of Enlightenment.

♫ The Sage, Gateshead

This stunning venue provides ample reason to get off at Newcastle if you're ever journeying up or down the East Coast mainline. If you already live in the North East of England, then you've really got no excuse for not having visited. The building is a marvel. Designed by Sir Norman Foster (his first performing arts venue, as it happens), The Sage, Gateshead, cost £70 million to construct. Most of the 3,858 tonnes of steel is hidden from view in the foundations; more than 11,000 steel piles were drilled into the round to support the massive structure; and more than 18,000 cubic metres of concrete were poured into the foundations of the building. That's enough concrete to fill 23 50-metre swimming pools. Inside, you'll find all sorts of music-making – from pensioners' workshops to parents' and babies' sessions – but if you're looking for an orchestral concert, you should make your way to

Hall One for a performance from Northern Sinfonia. This great group of musicians, led by their charismatic Music Director Thomas Zehetmair, is Classic FM's Orchestra in the North East of England.

♫ Glasgow Royal Concert Hall

'You've got a killer hall here.' So said the violinist Nigel Kennedy, no less, about the Glasgow Royal Concert Hall. It's Scotland's premier classical music venue and is the place to go for great live concerts in and around the city. The auditorium holds just shy of 2,500 seats and is often packed to bursting for performances from the Royal Scottish National Orchestra (Classic FM's Orchestra in Scotland). It is also the primary venue for 'Celtic Connections', the world's largest winter music festival, and the Hall hosts more than 400 concerts every year. It hasn't always been in such good shape, though. In the autumn of 1962, the then St Andrew's Halls were completely destroyed by fire. For the next 28 years, the city was without a concert hall, until the Glasgow Royal Concert Hall was opened in 1990.

♫ Town Hall and Symphony Hall, Birmingham

We've not cheated here by rolling two venues into one when they should, in fact, be separate. On the contrary, Town Hall and Symphony Hall are like twin brothers, albeit with the latter clearly acting as the bigger and louder of the two. Town Hall is definitely impressive in its own right, though. After all, any building whose design was based on the Roman temple of Castor and Pollux is clearly worthy of attention. Town Hall isn't just a concert venue; as the name suggests, it hosts all sorts of events with civic importance, from debates and speeches through to prime ministerial events (everyone from Gladstone to Thatcher has delivered a rallying cry there). There's no denying it, though: Town Hall is a beautiful venue for smaller-scale classical music concerts, while Symphony Hall's stunning acoustic makes it a perfect location for orchestral events. The City of Birmingham Symphony Orchestra (Sir Simon Rattle's old stomping ground) is resident there, and the venue regularly hosts prestigious orchestras and ensembles from abroad. Classic FM's Orchestra on Tour, the Philharmonia, is also a frequent visitor.

♫ Barbican Centre, London

The London Symphony Orchestra performs pretty much all of its UK concerts here – which is reason alone to ensure that the Barbican Centre is in our Top Ten list. When you add to that the fact that there are international residencies from the New York Philharmonic, Los Angeles Philharmonic, Leipzig Gewandhaus and Royal Concertgebouw Orchestras, the Barbican's inclusion is a dead cert. Described by the *Guardian* as 'a building where there is always something rich and strange going on', the Barbican Centre hosts a wealth of great classical music concerts as well as all sorts of visual art, dance and wider cultural events. There's a cinema, a library and a roof-top tropical conservatory alongside the 1,949-seat concert hall – all of which make a visit to the Barbican Centre whenever you're in London a very good idea indeed.

♫ Wales Millennium Centre, Cardiff

The Wales Millennium Centre – or, to give it its full Welsh name, the Canolfan Mileniwm Cymru – is a buzzing part of Cardiff's cultural scene, and a destination venue for audiences from miles around. Every year, over 500 performances of one kind or another take place there and the venue brings in £50 million to the Welsh economy; performers include the resident Welsh National Opera, as well as visiting orchestras and ensembles from across the globe. When the venue was commissioned, the architects Percy Thomas were instructed to create somewhere that was 'unmistakably Welsh and internationally outstanding'. It opened in 2004 and, along with St David's Hall up the road, the Wales Millennium Centre provides a compelling reason to make a trip to Cardiff for an unforgettable classical music experience.

♫ Royal Albert Hall, London

Of all the venues on our list, this is the one that probably needs the most minimal of introductions. Even if you've never been to the Royal Albert Hall, chances are it's already very much on your musical radar. The creation of the venue stretches all the way back to the days of Queen Victoria – or, more specifically, to her husband Prince

Albert, who believed that London needed a 'central hall' to promote the understanding and appreciation of the arts and sciences. Fast forward to the 21st century, and you'll find a place that hosts an eclectic and hugely enjoyable range of events – from Classic FM Live concerts to the Music for Youth Schools Proms, via all manner of pop, rock and jazz gigs.

♫ Bridgewater Hall, Manchester

The Hallé Orchestra is one of this country's finest ensembles, and their residency at Bridgewater Hall is one of a number of reasons for paying this remarkable venue a visit. It's a truly international concert hall: as well as its three resident UK orchestras, the Bridgewater Hall regularly hosts some of the finest musicians worldwide, and has a performance list that easily rivals the very best of the London concert halls. The first bricks of this striking structure were laid on 22nd March 1993, on a site that formerly housed a bus station and a rather unglamorous car-park. The most remarkable aspect of the building can be found right at the bottom. Somewhat bizarrely, the whole structure appears to float off the ground on almost 300 earthquake-proof giant springs, meaning that there is no actual link between the 22,500-tonne building and its foundations. Try not to think about that next time you're sitting there during a concert.

♫ Philharmonic Hall, Liverpool

This is the place to go if you want to hear the Royal Liverpool Philharmonic Orchestra (Classic FM's Orchestra in the North West of England) in action. This Grade II listed building dates from the 1930s. Nowadays, the 1,790-seat Art Deco concert hall is home not just to the RLPO, but to all sorts of ensembles – from jazz and folk to pop and rock. The RLPO gives around 70 concerts a year in this, its home venue, but if you want to hear them elsewhere in Liverpool, you'll often find the orchestra performing in the city's two cathedrals. They also regularly head further afield, performing across the UK – and around the world. While you're in Liverpool, you should also check out St George's Hall, just opposite Lime Street station. It's one of the most beautiful concert halls anywhere in the world and has even been designated a World Heritage site.

♫ Wigmore Hall, London

This is one of the UK's busiest concert venues, hosting in excess of 400 events every year, and it's a particularly great place to go if you like the idea of more intimate chamber music concerts and recitals, rather than the full-blown orchestral and operatic affairs available elsewhere. Completely restored in 2004, Wigmore Hall was built at the turn of the 20th century and was commissioned by the German piano-making firm Bechstein, who had a showroom on Wigmore Street and whose directors wanted a venue in which to showcase their wares. Wigmore Hall was designed by the same architect who created the rooms on a number of P&O cruise liners: one Thomas Colcott. It's a simply beautiful place. Concerts are held there nearly every lunchtime throughout the year, so if you happen to find yourself in Mayfair in the middle of the day and you have an hour to spare, this is most definitely the place to head.

CLASSICAL MUSIC'S TOP DOS AND DON'TS

Sadly, a great many people run a mile from classical music because they worry about how they should behave when they hear it. In jazz clubs, you know you can have a drink, chat away with those around you and be thoroughly relaxed; at a rock gig, it's frankly strange to sit there without moving; but in classical music, there still exists a perceived wisdom that if you don't remain rigid and silent, resembling residents at a mortuary, you're somehow doing something wrong.

It's important to remember that nearly all classical music was written to be enjoyed in a live setting. In the case of the vast majority of the great composers throughout history, their music was created years before radio, television or the internet had even been considered. In the minds of those who composed it, then, these sounds find their home in the concert venue: performers and their audience, together in the same room, gaining pleasure from giving and receiving brilliant music. Going to a concert should therefore ideally be the most natural experience in the world – not some kind of forced affair where you're made to feel guilty for smiling.

If you've never been to a classical music concert before and are thinking of giving it a go, here are a few dos and don'ts, which should help make your experience an even better one:

Do... wear whatever you want.
Years ago, you risked inducing a minor heart attack on the part of the man or woman sitting next to you if you turned up at a concert hall in anything less than formal evening wear. Thankfully, despite the many hackneyed pictures of classical music concerts, which depict them as rather prim and proper affairs, there's no need to wear anything other than what you're entirely comfortable in.

Do... take the opportunity to go to pre-concert talks.
There are some fascinating stories behind a great deal of classical pieces: love, death, betrayal and pretty much every other life experience under the sun have inspired composers to write some of their finest works. Finding out the stories behind the works themselves can make for a far more enriching experience once the music starts – and, in many venues, pre-concert talks are a perfect way of finding out everything you need to know. Usually free to fee-paying concert-goers, they often take the form of a brief talk from a musical expert, but at other times you'll get an interview with the conductor or musicians, or a question-and-answer session with the audience. And if you ever go to see the conductor Marin Alsop in action, do take the opportunity to go to one of her *post*-concert talks: she regularly stays on stage after the performance to field questions from the audience about what they've just heard. We think that more performers should follow her lead and stick around to talk to their audiences.

Do... go to a concert at a time that suits you.
Lots of ensembles put on commuter concerts in major cities on a regular basis. The City of Birmingham Symphony Orchestra has pioneered 'Rush Hour' concerts, which are held at around 6 p.m. and

last for no more than an hour. They're a great way to let go of the stresses and strains of the working day before heading home. In most cities, you can be pretty certain that a lunchtime concert is being held earlier that day. Elsewhere, meanwhile, you'll find a late-night concert by candlelight and, around the corner, there'll be a venue that hosts your traditional concert with an 8 o'clock start time. In other words, there's a concert to suit everyone's circumstances – so find the one that's right for you and give it a try.

Do... choose a concert based on what you want to hear, not what you think you should hear.

Many people just cannot stand opera. Too much singing, too many intervals, too much dying, and far too much looking up above you to read the translation of whatever that woman's singing about. For others, a concert of Baroque music leaves them cold: all those rigid structures, none of the heart-on-your-sleeve romance of Rachmaninov or Tchaikovsky. We all have our musical likes and dislikes, and it's crucially important not to see that as a problem. If you love summer pops concerts but your neighbour is more of an 'I don't feel alive until I've sat through a five-hour Wagner opera' sort of person, the chances are you'll both have a miserable time if you join the other at a concert one evening. Instead, you should feel no shame in going to what gives you pleasure.

Do... pay for the best seat you can afford.

As with any event, the better your view of the stage and the quality of the sound the more expensive the ticket will be. Make sure you've sussed out the venue in advance: you don't want to go to see your favourite star pianist only to discover that your seat is up in the gods with no view of his hands on the keyboard. The really cheap seats are cheap for a reason, and although you should still get a genuinely good experience in Row Y of the Upper Circle, it's worth occasionally treating yourself to a seat nearer the action if you're able to do so.

* * *

Don't... make too much noise.

This one really comes down to tradition: in the same way that it would be off-putting for a pop audience if you went around telling them all to be quiet, so it is inappropriate to make a great deal of noise in the wrong place at a classical concert. To quote the bassoon player John Steinmetz, 'There's nothing mysterious or difficult about how to act at a concert. It's mostly just common sense: the music needs silence, so the audience contributes silence; both the musicians and the audience want to concentrate on the music, so listeners stay put during a performance.' Consequently, chatting, texting, catching up on your emails, whispering (can anyone actually whisper quietly?) or unwrapping that bumper pack of Werther's Originals are all best avoided at a classical concert.

Don't... expect to be let in immediately if you turn up late.

If the concert you're going to starts with a 35-minute piano concerto, and you're two minutes late, chances are you'll have 33 minutes of hanging around with the bar staff while they get the interval orders ready. Unlike at the cinema, when you can slip in at the back only to discover that the adverts are still on anyway, classical music concerts don't tend to allow latecomers until a suitable gap in proceedings – and, given that classical pieces can be on the long side, it's definitely worth allowing yourself plenty of time to get to the venue.

Don't... clap whenever you like.

For many concert-goers, the notion of when to clap is a bit of a minefield. Don't you just start applauding when you like something? Surely, that's OK? Well, on one level it's fine – but if you're not careful, you can end up like the man with the enormous phone on *Trigger Happy TV* who makes a habit of standing up and shouting 'HELLO?' in the middle of the cinema. In other words, clapping can be really distracting, especially for those people around you who will be used to waiting until the whole 40-minute symphony is over before expressing their appreciation. It's complicated by the fact that in some classical music environments, applauding midway through is positively encouraged: during the opera, for example, it would be seen as rude not to clap the soloist at the end of an aria. But if you're attending the concert hall for the first time, you're best to wait until those around you start applauding before you jump to your feet and cheer.

Why, you might quite reasonably be wondering, should I not just clap when I feel the urge? Firstly, it can be distracting for the musicians: they want to give you the best possible experience; they want to feel you're involved and moved by the music, and if you clap halfway through the piece it can sometimes put them off. No one's going to be offended if you express your appreciation, but it's considerate to wait until the end of the piece. Secondly, although those around you may not look visibly moved, a great deal of emotion is often being stirred up underneath the surface – and if the person next to them starts making a noise, their experience of the concert can end up being a poorer one.

Don't... jump in at the deep end.
The journey of discovery through classical music is a marathon, not a sprint. Don't feel guilty for going along to concerts of really well-known repertoire: the pieces are well known because they're some of the most brilliant works ever written, and you don't need to feel bad for choosing a concert packed full of hits. There's plenty of time to discover 21st-century electro-acoustic compositions and five-hour piano recitals; for now, be encouraged to try out something entirely accessible, which you think you'll enjoy.

Don't... leave when the encore starts.
If the concert has gone well and everyone's cheering for more, the orchestra or soloist will quite often perform an unscheduled encore, usually lasting for not more than a couple of minutes. There are few things more disheartening for a musician than to see hordes of people get up and leave while they play their final piece – so, if you can, do stick around for a moment longer. It's nearly always worth the wait: classical music encores are usually incredibly impressive.

Don't... leave your mobile phone turned on.
If it rings in the middle of a performance, you will annoy everyone in

the concert hall, including the musicians on stage. In fact, 'outrage' might be a more accurate term than 'annoy'. And, on this one, we wholeheartedly agree with the most conservative of concert-goers. It's simple to check that your phone is turned off and it's rude to all concerned not to do so. If by some oversight your ringtone does echo around a concert hall, while you scrabble to find your handset in your bag, then switch it off straight away. On absolutely no account should you ever answer it during a performance. Classical concert-goers are by and large a peace-loving bunch, but nothing rouses them to ire more than a mobile phone going off midway through a beautiful slow movement. You have been warned!

* * *

Once you do go along to your first orchestral concert, you may well wonder exactly why the musicians are sat in that particular way on stage. It ultimately traces back to the French composer Jean-Baptiste Lully (see p77), whose court musicians were a precursor to the kind of modern orchestra we see today. Lully's band of merry men (and yes, it would have been solely men) consisted of around 24 players of stringed instruments, with the occasional woodwind player included for good measure.

As new instruments were invented, the orchestra inevitably grew in size, with percussion and brass eventually needing to be accommodated too. The same orchestral shape remained, though: a semi-circle of players, with the conductor placed at the front, in the centre.

Nowadays, you'll regularly find in excess of 100 orchestral musicians on stage, especially for large-scale works by the likes of Berlioz and Mahler. Quite some increase from the days of Lully's court musicians – but still very much the same principle: seat the musicians in a way that best conveys, to the audience, the sound that is being created.

Before we go on to recommend what you might like to include in your own classical music recording collection, a quick mention must be made for how you should go about choosing which performers to see live. After all, classical music isn't just about the repertoire: there are plenty of performances of Beethoven and Mozart that would cause the composers to turn in their graves. If the players aren't up to scratch then your concert-going experience will be a poor one, no matter how great the music is.

If you're looking for absolute musical excellence, you're safe to assume that the UK's major city symphony orchestras such as the Royal Liverpool Philharmonic, the Royal Scottish National, the Philharmonia or the Hallé will provide a very high standard of music-making.

Similarly, any soloists who appear with those ensembles are likely to be impressive. Another useful resource when it comes to well-known names is our website, classicfm.com, where you can find biographies of some of the most popular soloists, most of whom regularly perform in the UK.

Although all of these orchestras offer some excellent ticket offers, sometimes you can find that tickets cost up to £50 a throw, which can be hard to afford if you're operating on a tight budget. There are classical music events to suit every single income, and if you fancy some free music-making, why not head along to your local university music department or conservatoire? Performers learn by performing in front of an audience, and you'll be amazed at the standard of playing among the young people who study there. Local amateur orchestras and choral societies also provide good-value concerts, as do churches, small chamber groups and non-professional soloists. With so many concerts costing either nothing at all or very little to attend, you should find yourself able to try out plenty of different ones without burning a hole in your pocket.

Above all, go along to a live classical concert because you want to be entertained. It's there to be enjoyed – so let the composer and the performers enable you to do just that!

CHAPTER 3

YOUR OWN CLASSICAL MUSIC COLLECTION

First off, a bit of a disclaimer: parts of this chapter are unashamedly biased. Any book that recommends classical music recordings is going to be heavily shaped by personal opinion – and, chances are, not all of your opinions are the same as ours. In fact, you should have seen the in-depth discussions we had when it came to deciding what should or should not have made the list!

Over the next few pages, we'll point you towards what we believe are some of the best recordings of classical music – some because of their good value, others because of their unbeatable performances, and still more because they represent a milestone in the history of recorded music. The most important thing to say at the outset, though, is that you should feel liberated to buy whatever recordings give you pleasure. When it comes to deciding what to purchase with your own money, you are the only critic that matters.

We've gathered together all of the recommended recordings in this section – and also recommendations for each of the works we highlight throughout chapters 4 to 9 – online at www.classicfm.com/everything. Here, you'll find full details of the albums, along with links to download them from iTunes.

Before showcasing exactly which recordings we think are worthy of your attention and why, we'll take a whistle-stop tour through ten of the most important classical music labels, as well as endeavouring to guide you through the minefield that is the compilations market. Let's get started ...

THE CLASSICAL MUSIC LABELS THAT MATTER

Classical music is a broad church, and when it comes to record labels there's huge variety: major international companies such as Sony, Warner and Universal sit alongside organ music specialists, choral labels and those that exist solely to promote avant-garde contemporary music. There are outstanding recordings available on hundreds of different labels – but if you're starting out building a collection, these are well worth your initial attention. To avoid any accusations of favouring one label over another, we've put our list in a strictly alphabetical order.

♫ Chandos

Chandos is a family company, based in Colchester in Essex. It's known for championing esoteric repertoire alongside the more well-known names. When it started in 1979, Chandos made a name for itself by backing British composers, shining the spotlight on the likes of Arnold Bax and William Walton, whose music hadn't been given the profile it arguably deserved elsewhere.

Fast forward more than 30 years, and the Chandos back catalogue now numbers well over 2,000 different titles. Particularly good recordings to look out for on this label include anything from the violinist Tasmin Little, whose Elgar *Violin Concerto* with the Royal Scottish National Orchestra is just wonderful, and the Debussy piano music series with the amazing French pianist Jean-Efflam Bavouzet.

The Chandos strapline is 'Serious about Classical Music' – so you won't find many jazzy covers, jokey sleeve notes or controversial repertoire here. What you will find, though, is a label that's absolutely committed to a huge range of music, always performed to an extremely high standard.

♫ Decca

The Decca label has had an intriguing and impressive history: as well as being home to the likes of Luciano Pavarotti and Alfred Brendel, it was also the label of choice for Billie Holliday, Louis Armstrong and Judy Garland, among others. What's more, an entire website is dedicated to the Rolling Stones' Decca releases.

It's in classical music, though, that Decca has the richest heritage. Its roster has included greats such as the conductor Sir Georg Solti and the soprano Dame Joan Sutherland, along with the tenor Luciano Pavarotti. Indeed, it was Decca that released the astonishingly successful *Three Tenors* album in 1990. It introduced millions to classical music when Pavarotti joined with Placido Domingo and José Carreras to perform a host of operatic favourites.

Today, Decca exists in two distinct forms: Decca Classics, which, with its blue and red label, champions classical music artists such as the young pianists Benjamin Grosvenor and Behzod Abduraimov; while Decca Records, the black-labelled other half of the company includes everyone from crossover stars such as Alfie Boe, Noah Stewart and Hayley Westenra to artists from other genres such as Robert Plant, Imelda May and Melody Gardot.

In the UK classical music charts, Decca's mixture of pure classical and classical crossover stars, combined with its executives' canny knack of knowing exactly how to present each of its artists to the public, has meant that it has consistently been the best-performing label in commercial terms over the past decade.

♫ Deutsche Grammophon

Deutsche Grammophon – or DG as it's referred to by many – can lay claim to being not just the most important classical music label, but the most important label in the history of all recorded music. The reason? Founded in Hanover in 1898, Deutsche Grammophon was responsible for launching the world's first record and gramophone manufacturing works. Well over a century later, DG's prestigious yellow label has become shorthand for excellence and quality: its recordings may not always rank among the cheapest, but to this day its roster includes some of the world's finest classical musicians.

In 2009, the company released a beautiful 55-CD box set of some of their best ever recordings, to mark the label's 111th birthday. It's certainly not cheap, but if you're feeling flush then this is as wonderful a way as any to gain a fantastic audio history of classical music recordings from the turn of the 20th century to the present day.

Bryn Terfel, Anna Netrebko, Martha Argerich, Gustavo Dudamel, Magdalena Kožená, Anne-Sophie Mutter and Rolando Villazón are among the galaxy of international classical superstars signed to the label.

Like Decca, Deutsche Grammophon is part of the Universal Music Group.

♫ EMI Classics

EMI is home to all sorts of pop acts (not least of which, The Beatles), and it's perhaps most famous for opening the world's first purpose-built complex of recording studios way back in 1931, when the hitherto unknown address 3 Abbey Road began its transformation into an iconic location for recorded music. Like Deutsche Grammophon, EMI Classics has a history that dates back to the turn of the 20th century, when the label started out as a purveyor of music-hall artists and brass bands. A century later, and many of the world's most prestigious artists and orchestras have recorded for the label. Among them, great English conductors Sir Thomas Beecham and Sir Simon Rattle, the violinist Nigel Kennedy, and a host of operatic stars from Maria Callas to Angela Gheorghiu via Roberto Alagna and Placido Domingo.

In 2013, EMI was purchased by Universal Music as part of a major international take-over, but the record company's classical music division was sold on to Warner Classics, although the name 'EMI Classics' did not go with the sale. This has had the effect of dramatically increasing Warner's scale and influence in the classical world, given the enviable archive of great classical recordings that formed the EMI Classics back catalogue. Many of those original recordings have already been re-released with the Warner Classics logo replacing the familiar red EMI badge.

♫ Harmonia Mundi

Harmonia Mundi is the world's oldest independent record label: since 1958, this French company has championed classical music in all its glorious forms. In particular, Harmonia Mundi is known for releasing

Baroque music performed on period instruments of the kind that Bach and Handel would have played. It has also created some outstanding albums with the conductor René Jacobs, as well as with the British pianist Paul Lewis – whose Beethoven series won worldwide acclaim.

If you're wanting to buy albums that look as good on the coffee table as they sound on your speakers, Harmonia Mundi is always a good bet. Their discs are beautifully packaged with artwork, extensive sleeve notes and plenty of information about the performers – and, while they might not always be the cheapest on the market, they're certainly rewarding purchases.

Nowadays, Harmonia Mundi employs some 300 people around the world; its founder, the much loved Bernard Coutaz, died in 2010, and was succeeded by his daughter, Eva, who is now president of the company.

♫ Hyperion

The success and appeal of the Hyperion label lies in its quirkiness, its originality, and its discovery of some of the most remarkable repertoire. The founding of the company is fairly idiosyncratic: it was the brainchild of a music-loving taxi driver called Ted Perry, who launched Hyperion in 1980. Perry had worked in record shops as a young man and he saw a gap in the market for enjoyable, well-packaged classical music that was not necessarily well known.

British music has always been something of a Hyperion speciality: the label has unearthed all sorts of Scottish concertos, as well as championing contemporary British choral music and plenty of unknown works from the English Renaissance period. They have plenty of big names on their books, too, including the fantastic British pianist Stephen Hough, whose recording of all four Rachmaninov piano concertos with the Dallas Symphony Orchestra under Andrew Litton garnered five-star reviews from pretty much every classical music publication on the planet.

Despite its extensive back catalogue and worldwide acclaim, Hyperion remains a family company: Ted's son, Simon, now runs the business from an industrial estate in south-east London.

♫ Naxos

The philosophy of Naxos is quite different from that of all the other labels mentioned here: unlike its rivals, the company does not primarily focus on well-known names. Instead, Naxos is first and foremost a repertoire-driven company, providing recordings for people who often know what music they like but who don't necessarily mind by whom it's performed.

The company was founded in 1987 by an entrepreneur called Klaus Heymann; since then, the catalogue has expanded to nearly 5,000 separate titles. Every month, around 30 albums are released, and recording sessions take place in some 20 different countries every year. What's special about Naxos, though, is the price: in the UK, nearly all the company's classical albums sell for £5.99, which is less than half the price you would expect to pay for the same repertoire on many another labels.

When the company first started out, some of the performers on Naxos were less well known than those on some of the major labels. However, in recent years, Naxos has released some absolutely outstanding albums, which challenge that assumption. Not least among their critically acclaimed hits is the breathtaking series of Shostakovich symphonies with the Royal Liverpool Philharmonic Orchestra conducted by Vasily Petrenko.

♫ Sony Classical

As the label of choice for world-famous soloists such as the Chinese pianist Lang Lang and the American violinist Joshua Bell, Sony Classical is definitely worthy of your attention. When you add the fact that this is the label that champions modern-day film scores more than pretty much all the other major companies combined, Sony Classical becomes one of the most important players in all classical music.

The eighties was a golden time for Sony Classical: after the sale of the old CBS Masterworks label to the Sony Group, the company recorded albums with not just the film composer John Williams but the guitarist of the same name, too, as well as pianists Yevgeny Kissin and Murray Perahia and cellist Yo-Yo Ma.

Sony Classical's commitment to movie music is impressive: its release of *Titanic* made history in 1997 when it became the fastest-selling soundtrack ever – and, since then, the company has released the Oscar-winning music for *Crouching Tiger, Hidden Dragon, The Red Violin* and *Shakespeare in Love*.

♫ Virgin Classics

This Paris-based label was acquired by Warner Classics in 2013 and rebadged as Erato but, as its name would suggest, it was launched by Sir Richard Branson in the late 1980s. Virgin Classics was intended originally to be a label that profiled music rarely released by others – which is why, among its first ten discs, were one of 17th-century English viol music (a viol being a very early string instrument), another of the first ever period-instrument recording of Schubert's *Symphony No. 9*, and one more of orchestral music by the 20th-century British composer Michael Tippett.

In 1992, Virgin Classics became part of the EMI group – and, five years later, the label became permanently based in France. The label's A&R man (the person who discovers new artists), Alain Lanceron, has a reputation the world over for being very adept at finding new classical talent. In the last few years, the star young musicians he's introduced to Virgin Classics include pianist Alexandre Tharaud and the outstanding Quatuor Ebène string quartet. Virgin's releases are always beautifully packaged; for a label that's not even 25 years old yet, it already has a remarkable heritage of recordings.

♫ Warner Classics

Until its acquisition of the EMI Classics and Virgin Classics labels, Warner Classics was predominantly a back-catalogue company, providing excellent value-for-money compilations and reissues. It's also seen some great successes in the classical download market, becoming one of the first labels to truly understand the importance of targeting a generation of classical music enthusiasts who don't necessarily want to buy a physical CD. Alongside the back-catalogue and digital achievements, Warner Classics does still sign new artists: in 2011, they released a successful album of Romantic concertos with the young violinist Charlie Siem, while in 2012 they embraced the genre of classical crossover with a new album from the million-copy-selling Opera Babes. And if you fancy some Russian discoveries, try the brilliant set of Glazunov symphonies which Warner Classics has released over the last few years, featuring the Royal Scottish National Orchestra conducted by José Serebrier.

WHAT ABOUT COMPILATIONS?

Despite what some of the critics might say, and no matter how many people turn their noses up at the idea, classical music compilation albums are often a brilliant way to get started on building your own collection. One word of advice, though: where possible, avoid the ones in motorway service stations. Yes, they might cost only the very special price of just £3 when you also buy a premium car wash, but quality is not their middle name.

What you won't get with a compilation is lots of information about the composer, the performers, or the music. But then, that's not necessarily a bad thing. It all comes down to what you want, and how you fancy going about exploring the world of classical music. Artist-led albums are still a crucial part of any classical music journey – but that journey can definitely begin with compilation collections.

So, what to recommend? Quite often, compilations are grouped by mood: we have our own *Smooth Classics* sets at Classic FM, while other labels excel in 'driving classics', film music, even 'football classics'. If you particularly enjoy listening to laid-back classical music, there is a wealth of albums available to you; if in doubt, choose one from one of the labels recommended above, as a guarantee that you're buying a quality product. Many of the compilations from the likes of Decca and Sony Classical include tracks performed by world-famous soloists – so, even if you're not getting the whole concerto or symphony, you can be sure that what you're buying contains very high-quality music-making.

Our own Classic FM Full Works range includes a number of compilations, alongside complete recordings from the Decca and Deutsche Grammophon back-catalogue. You can find out more online at classicfm.com/fullworks.

At the moment, the vast majority of classical music sales in the UK are still on CDs. But we can expect that to change, as digital downloads take an ever bigger slice of the recording pie each year. Record companies are increasingly working with the main online stores such as iTunes and Amazon to find new ways of packaging classical music tracks together to help those people who are starting to build their collections. Although sales of compilation CDs have fallen in recent years, it's quite conceivable that record companies will come up with a new way of putting together digital compilations in the future, which could see this way of buying music rise to the fore once again.

We try our best to provide purchasing links to every track we play on the radio, on our website at classicfm.com/playlist.

RECOMMENDATIONS

Over the remaining pages of this chapter, we'll delve into the rich history of recorded music and pick out some of the best recommendations for you to explore for yourself. The albums we've chosen aren't necessary the most seminal, but they're certainly perfect for any beginner.

For example, although Rachmaninov's own recording of his *Piano Concerto No. 2* is a thrilling historical record and is certainly worth listening to, it's not the version we would recommend to someone who had heard the piece on Classic FM and wanted to get hold of a copy for the first time – not least because it was recorded nearly 100 years ago and the audio quality just isn't of the kind that most people would find acceptable in today's hi-fidelity digital world.

What's more, we've focused on only the really major, well-known classical composers and works here. With a finite amount of space, preference is given to composers such as Bach, Mozart and Tchaikovsky over the likes of Berlioz, Delius and Gounod. In the next part of the book, we do make further recommendations of each featured composer's main work – and you can also cross-reference this with the Classic FM Hall of Fame list in the third part of the book. So, we hope you will find plenty of pointers within these pages to help you go off on your own journey of discovery.

Do also bear in mind that there are a huge number of suggestions online at classicfm.com, should our selections whet your appetite for more.

We've also deliberately left out recordings of full operas, in part because we recommend going and seeing an opera live before trying to appreciate it on disc. That's not to say you can't enjoy these recordings, but that we feel that somebody who's looking to start his or her classical collection from scratch should probably not dive into full-length operatic repertoire in the first instance.

Below, then, in alphabetical order by composer, is a rundown of what we would say are some of the best albums to purchase if you want to start exploring classical recordings for yourself.

♫ J. S. Bach

Bach's *48 Preludes and Fugues* laid the foundations for so much of what was to follow in classical music history; pretty much every great composer was inspired by them in some way. We love the recordings by Angela Hewitt (Hyperion) and Daniel Barenboim (Warner Classics), both of which bring a freshness and a faithfulness of which the composer would have surely approved.

Other fine Bach must-haves include a recording of the *Brandenburg Concertos*; the version by the European Brandenburg Ensemble, conducted by Trevor Pinnock, is just outstanding. It was released on the Avie label in 2007, and is a joy to listen to from start to finish.

Bach's vocal music is also worth a delve – try The Sixteen's version of the *Mass in B minor* on the Coro label. Then there's the keyboard concertos: Angela Hewitt on Hyperion is once again a good bet – she plays Bach better than most other people combined. And for the best ever recording of the beautiful *Cello Suites*, it's another Hyperion recommendation – this time from the soloist Steven Isserlis, who plays with wonderful style and grace.

♫ Beethoven

Where on earth do we begin with Beethoven? The man changed classical music for ever, wrote the most famous four notes in the history of classical music (the 'da-da-da DAAAAAH' at the start of *Symphony No. 5*, in case you're wondering), and can't possibly be distilled into a couple of paragraphs when it comes to the entire back catalogue of his music. However, there are definitely a few essentials.

Investing in a set of all nine symphonies is a very good idea: as well as that famous Fifth, there's also the *'Pastoral'* (*No. 6*), the *'Eroica'* (*No. 3*) and the mighty *No. 9* (*'Choral'*), which includes the famous *'Ode to Joy'*. There are some great recordings of individual symphonies, including *No. 5*, from Otto Klemperer on EMI Classics. In the 1960s, his performances with the Philharmonia Orchestra drew huge crowds at the Royal Festival Hall, and you can sense some of that excitement on disc. In terms of complete sets, there are good ones released in recent years from the Leipzig Gewandhaus Orchestra conducted by Riccardo Chailly on Decca, as well as Sir Simon Rattle and the Berlin Philharmonic Orchestra on EMI Classics. But our personal favourite is Christian Thielemann with the Vienna Philharmonic Orchestra on Sony Classical, released in January 2012, and featuring the most astonishing playing and beautiful sound quality.

If Beethoven's your man, you also need to get hold of some of his piano music. The complete concertos have been recorded by most of the big-name soloists: the American pianist Richard Goode collaborated with the Budapest Festival Orchestra conducted by Iván Fischer in a set that is hard to better; it's available on the Nonesuch label. Other good versions include one by Howard Shelley. His autumn 2011 release on Chandos saw him directing the Orchestra of Opera North from the keyboard in everything Beethoven wrote for piano and orchestra. And for a favourite from the 1980s, which still stands up to scrutiny today, try the Chilean pianist Claudio Arrau's version of the most famous *Piano Concerto No. 5* (*'Emperor'*), on the Philips label. He's brilliantly accompanied by Staatskapelle Dresden, under the baton of Sir Colin Davis.

All 32 Beethoven piano sonatas, meanwhile, have been recorded by most pianists worth their salt. Mitsuko Uchida's beautiful collection, again on Philips, is a real winner; we're also keeping a close eye on the young pianist HJ Lim, who released her first Beethoven sonatas disc in January 2012 on EMI Classics and who is being tipped as one of the star pianists of the future. Will her set become a must-have? Only time will tell.

Finally, the Beethoven *Violin Concerto* is another masterpiece that deserves a place on your shelf or your mp3 player. There are all sorts of remarkable historic recordings of the piece – among them, the great violinist Yehudi Menuhin with the equally great conductor Wilhelm Furtwängler, available on EMI Classics' *Great Recordings of the Century* range (which, incidentally, is well worth exploring for other gems). Fine performances in modern-day stereo sound include our current favourite: Vadim Repin alongside the Vienna Philharmonic Orchestra conducted by Riccardo Muti, available on Deutsche Grammophon.

♫ Brahms

The four Brahms symphonies, which weren't written until the composer was into his forties, are sublime from start to finish. Contrary to popular belief, Brahms didn't intend them to be performed by a huge orchestra, which is what makes Sir Charles Mackerras's version with the Scottish Chamber Orchestra, on the Telarc label, so special. There's a pared-down, precise sound here, which really seems to reach into the heart of what Brahms was trying to communicate. Have a listen, and experience romance in pretty much every bar of music.

If you enjoy those, make sure you then invest in the late Brahms *Intermezzi*, given a beautiful performance by Leif Ove Andsnes on the EMI Classics label. On Deutsche Grammophon you'll find a marvellous recording of *Piano Concerto No. 1*, played by Maurizio Pollini with Staatskapelle Dresden conducted by Christian Thielemann, while on Virgin Classics there's a thrilling take on *Piano Concerto No. 2* from the young pianist Nicholas Angelich, accompanied by the Frankfurt Radio Symphony Orchestra conducted by Paavo Järvi.

Finally, Brahms's *A German Requiem* is a heavenly piece of music when performed well – and, again, it's the Frankfurt Radio Symphony Orchestra under Paavo Järvi on Virgin Classics who get the recommendation here. The singing is simply sensational, from soloists including the soprano Natalie Dessay, and from the excellent Swedish Radio Choir.

♫ Bruch

The real must-own when it comes to Bruch is his *Violin Concerto No. 1*. Our favourite performance of this former Number 1 in the Classic FM Hall of Fame (our annual poll of the nation's favourite classical music) comes from a violinist who's not that well known but whose playing is phenomenal. His name: Vadim Gluzman. This recording sees him joined by the Bergen Philharmonic Orchestra conducted by Andrew Litton, and it's available on the Swedish label BIS. For a very different but equally illuminating performance, try the 15-year-old Yehudi Menuhin alongside the London Symphony Orchestra. It's available on the bargain-priced Naxos label, as part of its Historical Great Violinists series.

♫ Chopin

Continuing the 'how can he be that good when he's still just a boy?' theme, Yevgeny Kissin's recording of the Chopin *Piano Concertos* is worth you lending your ears to if only because he was just twelve years old when they were recorded. Yes, that's right. *Twelve*. Think about what you were doing at that age when you listen to these performances; they're by no means perfect, but they're still astonishing in their own right. The album is available on the RCA Victor label and was recorded live in concert in Moscow.

Our favourite recording of the two Chopin *Piano Concertos*, though, comes from Martha Argerich. She first recorded them both for Deutsche Grammophon in the 1970s, but our pick is her EMI Classics release with the Montreal Symphony Orchestra and the conductor Charles Dutoit. Simply gorgeous playing in every bar, guaranteed to hook you in and make you feel better about life with every listen.

There are stacks of other fine pianists who tackle Chopin's solo works with grace and aplomb – among them, Stephen Hough, Nikolai Lugansky and Ingrid Fliter – but any Chopin fan really needs at least one album from the great Maurizio Pollini. Pollini turned 70 in January 2012, when a 3-CD tribute set was released by his label Deutsche Grammophon. Called *The Art of Maurizio Pollini*, it includes the whole of Chopin's *Piano Concerto No. 1*, alongside the *Etudes* and a couple of *Polonaises*. Definitely one to add to your Christmas list.

♫ Debussy

Here's another master of piano music – although his sound is very different from that of Chopin. Debussy's dreamy, Impressionistic soundscapes are wonderfully played by the British pianist Kathryn Stott. Her budget-priced recording of the *Suite Bergamasque* (from which the famous *'Clair de Lune'* is taken) is available on the Sony Essential Masterworks series.

In terms of orchestral music, Debussy's hazy *Prélude à l'après midi d'un faune* is performed expertly by the Cleveland Orchestra under the baton of Vladimir Ashkenazy. What's more, at the turn of the 21st century the Decca label released this recording on a disc that also includes arguably the best ever interpretation of the composer's *La Mer* – and it retails for just a fiver nowadays. Bargain!

♫ Dvořák

Dvořák's famous *Symphony No. 9* (*'From the New World'*) is his most popular work, and the performances don't get much better than the one from Fritz Reiner and the Chicago Symphony Orchestra on the RCA label. Other Dvořák gems include the *Cello Concerto*. Yo-Yo Ma gives an intense and thrilling take with the New York Philharmonic Orchestra on Sony Classical but, for many people, Jacqueline du Pré's recording with the Royal Liverpool Philharmonic Orchestra under conductor Sir Charles Groves, recorded in 1969 and released by BBC Legends, cannot be bettered.

♫ Elgar

Time to recommend Jacqueline du Pré once more: her recording of the Elgar *Cello Concerto* is a piece of classical music history. Du Pré is at her best alongside Sir John Barbirolli and the London Symphony Orchestra, on a recording on the EMI Masters range; Barbirolli himself was a cello player in the orchestra at the 1919 premiere of the work, so he obviously knew how it should sound.

The other Elgar essential is the *Enigma Variations*: we always return to the LSO Live release profiling the London Symphony Orchestra once more, this time conducted by Sir Colin Davis. And finally, a quick reminder of Tasmin Little's extraordinarily beautiful recording of the Elgar *Violin Concerto* with the Royal Scottish National Orchestra conducted by Sir Andrew Davis on Chandos. It won the Critics' Choice Award at the Classic BRIT Awards in 2011, and it will certainly stand the test of time for many decades to come.

♫ Górecki

The Polish composer Henryk Górecki shot to fame in the early 1990s as a result of the sudden popularity of his *Symphony No. 3* (*'Symphony of Sorrowful Songs'*). The album became a million-seller: a great result for this reclusive composer, and a welcome profits boost for his label Nonesuch. Soprano Dawn Upshaw is joined by the London Sinfonietta conducted by David Zinman; this album certainly isn't an essential one if you're just discovering classical music, but is a good one to try once you've explored works by other more familiar composers.

♫ Grieg

There are lots of fine works by Grieg – among them, the *Holberg Suite*, the sets of *Lyric Pieces* and the *Symphonic Dances* – but the one piece that towers above them all is the composer's *Piano Concerto*, made forever famous by Morecambe and Wise and André 'Andrew Preview' Previn. In our opinion, Krystian Zimmerman's Deutsche Grammophon recording, with the Berlin Philharmonic Orchestra conducted by Herbert von Karajan, has yet to be bettered. What's more, the disc also includes the heavenly Schumann *Piano Concerto*, giving you well over an hour of beautiful Romantic music on one album.

♫ Handel

Handel's *Messiah* includes favourite choruses such as *'For Unto Us a Child is Born'* and the *'Hallelujah Chorus'*. There are literally hundreds of recordings of the work. Our favourite one was released in 2009, to commemorate both the 250th anniversary of the composer's death and the 800th birthday of the University of Cambridge. Not surprisingly, then, it features the Choir of King's College, Cambridge, and a quartet of fine soloists, all conducted by Nicholas Cleobury. It was released on EMI Classics in both CD and DVD format (as well as digital download, of course) and the whole performance exudes joy from start to finish.

If you're more of an instrumental music fan, try Handel's *Music for the Royal Fireworks*, given a great, zesty interpretation by the Baroque period band Zefiro on the Harmonia Mundi label.

♫ Haydn

Haydn composed 104 symphonies, which inevitably means that there are rather a lot of recordings of his orchestral music. Our pick of the best includes René Jacobs conducting the Freiburg Baroque Orchestra for Harmonia Mundi, as well as Nikolaus Harnoncourt's *'Paris' Symphonies* set with Concentus Musicus Vienna – also on Harmonia Mundi. Or, if you're feeling flush, try the excellent Hyperion box set of Haydn's late symphonies featuring the Orchestra of Italian Switzerland conducted by Howard Shelley.

In terms of another big Haydn hit, mention must be made of the *Trumpet Concerto*. Often paired on recordings with Hummel's concerto for the instrument, you won't go far wrong if you get hold of John Wallace's version in a recording that features no fewer than five separate works. He's joined by the Philharmonia Orchestra conducted by Christopher Warren-Green, and you'll find it on the Nimbus label.

♫ Mozart

Where on earth do we begin with Mozart? The most popular composer in classical music has an unrivalled back catalogue to his name – but here are the recordings that we think you should definitely invest in.

The composer's *Clarinet Concerto* is his most popular piece of music and is performed in the most beautiful, autumnal way by the British clarinettist Thea King alongside the English Chamber Orchestra conducted by Jeffrey Tate. It was one of the first recordings released by the Hyperion label and it remains one of the best they've ever put together.

In the case of the 41 symphonies, Mozart definitely saved the best till last, and the Scottish Chamber Orchestra's recordings of *Nos. 38–41* with conductor Sir Charles Mackerras on the Linn label are buzzing with life, wit and melody. And when it comes to the 27 piano concertos, there's a similar case of Mozart keeping his best tunes until the end. In the right hands, *Nos. 20–27* are packed to bursting with ebullience – and we'd recommend you explore the recordings by Alfred Brendel first and foremost. Other fine pianists who have tackled these works with resounding success include Mitsuko Uchida, Imogen Cooper and Daniel Barenboim.

Finally, fans of choral music should look no further than the Mozart *Requiem* – and, in particular, the version featuring soprano Emma Kirkby and the Academy of Ancient Music on Decca. Simply divine.

♫ Rachmaninov

Rachmaninov's *Piano Concerto No. 2* is one of the world's most popular pieces of music, not least because of its use in the movie *Brief Encounter*, but the composer wrote four concertos for the instrument in total. You might initially think you really need a recording only of *No. 2* – but wait until you hear Stephen Hough playing them all, with the bonus addition of the *Rhapsody on a Theme of Paganini*, and you'll quickly find the whole set to be indispensable. Featuring Hough alongside the Dallas Symphony Orchestra under Andrew Litton, and all captured live in concert, this thrilling set is an absolute winner.

If you're a fan of great Russian Romantic music, you might also like to invest in a recording of Rachmaninov's *Symphony No. 2*, and recordings don't come better than the one from conductor Sir Antonio Pappano and his Santa Cecilia Orchestra, released by EMI Classics. The fiendishly difficult *Preludes* for solo piano, meanwhile, are performed by Vladimir Ashkenazy as if his life depended on it; this one's available on a bargain-priced 2-CD Decca set.

♫ Schubert

For a perfect example of a well-crafted and tune-packed symphony, try Schubert's evergreen *Symphony No. 5*. All four movements feature melody after melody, and the performance from the Academy of St Martin in the Fields conducted by Sir Neville Marriner is a particular corker. It's available as a single CD – but also as part of an incredibly good-value box set from Newton Classics which, for under £30, gives you all nine Schubert symphonies spread across six

CDs, alongside a couple of other orchestral works that the composer never completed.

♫ Johann Strauss Jnr

How do you take your Strauss? Do you like it played with as much glitz, glamour, reverb and rubato as possible? If so, André Rieu is the man for you. This Dutch showman has introduced the Strauss waltz to millions of people across the world, who adore his buoyant approach and his willingness to have fun with the music. Rieu is a million-seller for his record label, Decca, and his albums *Moonlight Serenade* and *Forever Vienna* are hugely popular. He's done great things to emphasise the unstuffy nature of classical music, and he should be applauded for igniting a love for all things Strauss among people who had never fully appreciated these great dances before.

If, however, you find the big Rieu sound all a bit too much, try one of the New Year's Day concerts released by Sony Classical. The 2011 one is particularly good: it sees the Vienna Philharmonic Orchestra conducted by Franz Welser-Möst, and includes all the Strauss favourites – not least *By the Beautiful Blue Danube* and, from Johann Strauss Snr, the toe-tapping *Radetzky March*.

♫ Tchaikovsky

Another composer who manages to exude melody with everything he writes, Tchaikovsky was an absolute master of orchestration, using every instrument to thrilling effect. Very often, the best recordings of his music are by his fellow Russians – especially in the case of the symphonies. Try Valery Gergiev and the Kirov Orchestra's *Symphony No. 6 ('Pathetique')* on the Philips label and you'll be instantly won over by the rich, almost chocolatey string sound.

Another Russian conductor, Vasily Petrenko, has recorded a great album of Tchaikovsky ballet highlights with the Royal Liverpool Philharmonic Orchestra; it's available on Avie Records.

Tchaikovsky's *Piano Concerto No. 1*, meanwhile, is, quite simply, one of the finest concertos ever composed. It's brilliantly played by Stephen Hough on a Hyperion recording, which also includes Tchaikovsky's other two piano concertos. The other Tchaikovsky concerto of note is his one for the violin. There are many fine historic recordings of this, but we've fallen in love with the one from young soloist Valeriy Sokolov, released on Virgin Classics in 2011.

♫ Vaughan Williams

Until 2011, Nigel Kennedy's recording of *The Lark Ascending* with the City of Birmingham Symphony Orchestra conducted by Sir Simon Rattle seemed as if it would forever hold the status as the must-have recording of the piece. Then, along came violin sensation Julia Fischer, with her gorgeous album on Decca featuring the Orchestre Philharmonique de Monte Carlo conducted by Yakov Kreizberg. In Fischer's recording, the lark seems to soar higher than ever before; the album was made all the more poignant by the fact that, shortly after it was recorded, Yakov Kreizberg lost his brave battle with cancer.

Other fine Vaughan Williams albums to get you started include one called *English Fantasia*, which is a repackaged, budget-priced release in the Sony Essential Masterworks range. All the performances are from the Britten Sinfonia conducted by Nicholas Cleobury; you get the *Fantasia on Greensleeves*, the *Fantasia on a Theme by Thomas Tallis*, and more orchestral music by Elgar and Delius.

♫ Verdi

Verdi's fiery *Requiem* is a thrill from start to finish, and the full-blooded Italian performance given to it by the Orchestra and Chorus of Santa Cecilia conducted by Sir Antonio Pappano is absolutely electrifying. It's available on EMI Classics, and features an all-star line-up of soloists including tenor Rolando Villazón and bass René Pape.

A BRIEF H

CLASSIC

So far in this book, we've set out some of the terminological tools to help you better understand how classical music works; we've shared our tips for enjoying the music itself, whether on a recording or live in the concert hall, and we've given you some pointers as to the great performers. But, at the moment, we haven't necessarily always given you the context of where different composers and pieces of classical music have come in the history of the genre.

In the third part of this book, you'll find a handy chronological guide to composers' lives and achievements, so that you can gain an idea of who was around at the same time.

But first, in the next six chapters, we want to take you through classical music in a more narrative form. As we said at the beginning, this isn't going to be the most detailed history of classical music you can lay your hands on, but we think that it will provide you with an excellent basis of knowledge on which you can build in the future. In fact, towards the back of the book, there's a chapter with a few ideas to help you do just that.

We're going to journey through more than 1,000 years of music-making in fewer than 120 pages. Along the way, we'll visit the different eras of classical music, highlighting the main musical developments and picking out the significant composers of each period. We'll also make recommendations of the major works from each composer's output, allowing you to delve into the music of the ones you like to find out more.

Although our survey is arranged broadly in order of the years the composers were born, we have sometimes grouped together composers who shared a particular aspect – such as nationality, approach or genre – to make the changing musical styles clearer.

It's a bit of a romp, so fasten your seatbelt ... it's well worth the ride!

CHAPTER 4

EARLY MUSIC

IN THE BEGINNING

Music has been around for a long time. Historians have no doubt about that, although there are differing opinions about exactly when and where the idea of making musical instruments to play tunes first took hold. Fragments of primitive instruments, crafted more than ten centuries ago, have been found by archaeologists in places as far apart as Germany, Spain, Egypt and China.

Human beings are inherently musical. We can make all sorts of sounds with just our bodies, and the earliest musicians probably had no need for instrumental add-ons at all. Singing, clapping and even foot tapping are all forms of music. In fact, they are used today as a means of teaching very young children about the rudiments of making music.

When we talk about **Early Music** in the classical music world, we have a fairly clear idea about what we mean. It's not necessarily the earliest music known to humankind. Instead, the term tends to be used to describe the earliest forms of Western classical music, composed principally between 1000 and 1600, covering the **Medieval** and **Renaissance** periods.

WHAT ELSE WAS GOING ON IN THE WORLD?

Well, in the year 985 or 986, the Viking Bjarni Herjolfsson was blown off course and sighted the coast of America. The continent was not discovered officially by a European for just over 500 years, when Christopher Columbus landed in the West Indies in 1492.

The dawning of the second millennium saw England under attack from the Danes. In 1012, the invading forces rampaged through Canterbury, although they were bought off with 48,000 pounds of silver.

King Canute ruled England from 1016 to 1035 and King Harold was briefly on the throne in 1066 until William the Conqueror took over the crown following the Battle of Hastings. Scotland's kings included Macbeth from 1040 to 1057.

In fact, what we consider now to be **Early Music** was composed right through the time that England was reigned over by members of the House of Plantagenet (1154–1399), the House of Lancaster (1399–1461), the House of York (1461–1485) and the House of Tudor, ending with the reign of Elizabeth I between 1558 and 1603. In Scotland, James VI was on the throne from 1567, becoming James I of England following Elizabeth I's death in 1603.

This period encompasses the Crusades, the signing of the Magna Carta, the devastating scourge of the Black Death across Europe and the Hundred Years War between Britain and France, from 1337 to 1453.

So, the world was a busy place, with warfare at the top of many people's agendas as one tribe or nation plotted to take over another, only to find their efforts reversed a few years later. However, as you will see, there were huge developments in music, many of which were brought about by the Catholic Church.

AMBROSE AND GREGORY

Although the title above sounds like a 1970s television sitcom, Ambrose was in fact Bishop of Milan between 374 and 397; and Gregory I was Pope between 590 and 604. Among the latter's many claims to fame was his decision to send Augustine to England to convert the locals to Christianity.

Bishop Ambrose and Pope Gregory are generally credited with making great strides in the evolution of **plainsong**, which was the unaccompanied singing that took place as part of church services, most often performed by monks.

Ambrose was an important figure in the development of **antiphonal** singing, where two parts of a choir sing alternately with the second section answering the first. Gregory's contribution is, however, more often remembered by musical historians, and he is given the credit for a more general overhaul of this area of music a couple of hundred years later. He gave his name to the result, and Gregorian Chant was born.

HITTING THE RIGHT NOTE

People had been trying to write down music for a while by the start of the second millennium, but there was no truly uniform method for making a record of exactly who had to sing what and when, and for how long.

We know that instrumental music was also being made in the centuries before the end of the first millennium, but there is no accurate record of what sort of tunes were being composed, so we can only imagine how they might have sounded.

In around 1025, a monk called Guido d'Arezzo published his theories on musical notation. He had developed a system that meant chants could be read and then sung by anyone who had learned to decipher the code that he had created. Today, we call this deciphering 'reading music'.

For this reason, we are able to understand and give authentic performances of music written 1000 years ago. It means that the heritage of classical music has been preserved in a way that other musical genres from around the world simply have not been. We have a lot to thank Guido d'Arezzo for.

THE REALLY EARLY COMPOSERS

The first composer in this era is a woman. She is, in fact, the only female composer featured with anything other than a walk-on part in the whole of this book. If you read through the list of the Top 300 works in the Classic FM Hall of Fame on pages 193–201, you will notice that no pieces by women feature among our listeners' favourites.

✦ AT A GLANCE ✦

HILDEGARD OF BINGEN
BORN: 1098
DIED: 1179
NATIONALITY: GERMAN
MUST LISTEN: *A FEATHER ON THE BREATH OF GOD*

But that does nothing to take away from the achievements of **Hildegard of Bingen**. Although she was born into a noble family in 1098, she was sent away to a monastery at the age of just eight. By the time she was 38, she had become the leader of the nuns who were based at the monastery and, around 12 years later, she founded her own nunnery near the town of Bingen.

Hildegard was no ordinary nun. Apart from having a gift for writing poetry and music, she became an influential diplomat, corresponding regularly with religious and secular leaders. As a thinker, she made her name in areas such as science and medicine.

Hildegard became famed as a mystic and, between 1141 and 1170, she had no fewer than 26 visions. She wrote down their details and set them to music.

People travelled from far and wide to consult Hildegard, and when she died at the age of 81 (a remarkable achievement in itself at the time), the Catholic Church considered making her a saint, although she was never actually canonised. Some recent reports from Rome suggest that the current Pope may make this happen before too long.

Some composers lived for the moment and others spent their time worrying about their legacy. **Guillaume de Machaut** was firmly in the latter camp, although he was not without talent: he counted Geoffrey Chaucer among his fans. Machaut was one of the 'Ars Nova' composers who were responsible for many innovations in French and Italian classical music during the 1300s. In particular, he is remembered for developing new ways of using rhythms.

+ AT A GLANCE +

GUILLAUME DE MACHAUT
BORN: AROUND 1300
DIED: 1377
NATIONALITY: FRENCH
MUST LISTEN: *MESSE DE NOTRE DAME* –
HIS FAMOUS FOUR-PART MASS

Machaut became a canon in Rheims when he was about 40, and he seems to have spent much of the rest of his life bossing around the monks who were instructed to reproduce copies of his complete works. His desire for musical immortality was not in vain and he is one of the best-known composers of the period, simply because so much of his music still survives.

Although he was a priest, this doesn't seem to have stopped Machaut writing extensively on the subject of unfulfilled passion, and many of his songs were not religious at all. Instead, he adopted the style of the troubadours, wandering poets and musicians who performed their work in the homes of the French nobility.

However, it's for his four-part *Mass* that Machaut is most respected. He was among the first composers to write four separate tunes for people with different voices, which combined together harmoniously, and this was a big step forward in the history of classical music. This new style of singing was known as **polyphony**.

THE RENAISSANCE MEN

As you will discover as our story unfolds, there are periods in the history of classical music where similar developments occurred simultaneously in different countries.

One of the big times of change in the type of classical music that was written was what we now call the **Renaissance Period**. Literally translated from the French, *renaissance* means 'rebirth'. The British tend to think of **John Dunstable** as heading up their group (or 'school') of Renaissance composers, while in France, it was the Belgian **Guillaume Dufay** who was carrying the torch for the rebirth.

+ AT A GLANCE +

JOHN DUNSTABLE
BORN: AROUND 1390
DIED: 1453
NATIONALITY: ENGLISH
MUST LISTEN: *PRECO PREHEMINENCIE*

The Renaissance was not just going on in the world of music; the new discoveries also spanned science, exploration and the visual arts.

John Dunstable was one of English music's greatest exports and, rather like The Beatles in the 1960s, he was very much the face of English music abroad in the mid-1400s. Composers around Europe were impressed by his style of writing, and incorporated many of his new ideas into their own compositions. All of this popularity led to Dunstable becoming something of a property magnate back home, with a string of houses to his name across the south of England.

Almost all of the music Dunstable wrote was for use in the church, and he managed to create a particularly rich sound. Guillaume Dufay was one of the Continental composers who was influenced by Dunstable's music.

+ AT A GLANCE +

GUILLAUME DUFAY
BORN: AROUND 1397
DIED: 1474
NATIONALITY: BELGIAN
MUST LISTEN: *MASSE 'L'HOMME ARMÉ'*

Dufay was the illegitmate son of a priest and began his musical career as a boy chorister at Cambrai Cathedral. He moved on to Bologna in Italy and worked for the Pope in Rome and Florence. In the 1450s,

Dufay composed a Mass based on a folk song called *'L'Homme armé'*, which translates as *'The Armed Man'*. He was one of a long line of composers in musical history to use this title for a Mass – the most recent of whom is the Welshman Karl Jenkins, whose *The Armed Man (A Mass for Peace)* was premiered in 2000.

Dufay wrote every sort of music that had been invented at the time, including a wide variety of religious music and a range of secular songs. Word has it that he was also the first composer to write a Requiem Mass, but this is hard to prove definitively because the manuscript has been lost in the passage of time.

✦ AT A GLANCE ✦

JOHN TAVERNER
BORN: AROUND 1490
DIED: 1545
NATIONALITY: ENGLISH
MUST LISTEN: *MASS 'THE WESTERN WYNDE'*
FOR FOUR VOICES

Now, it's easy to become confused about our next composer, **John Taverner**. Don't mistake him for John Tavener (without the extra 'r'), who is alive today and composing music as you read this. We will come to him much later on in Chapter 9.

John Taverner was one of the big stars of English music in this period. As well as being a composer, he was a friend of Thomas Cromwell, one of the main forces behind the dissolution of the monasteries. It is possible that Taverner was a supporter of these reforms; he is on record as saying that he was embarrassed to have penned 'popish ditties' early on in his career as a composer. This idea is explored in a 1970 opera called *Taverner*, which was written by Sir Peter Maxwell Davies, who is now the Master of the Queen's Music. Again, more on him much later on in this book (see Chapter 9).

Thomas Tallis was another mighty force in English music. He was composing throughout the reigns of Henry VIII, who broke away from Rome and created the Church of England; Edward VI; Mary I, who was Catholic; and Elizabeth I, who was Protestant. Considering that Tallis managed to write music for the Church during all four of these reigns, he must have been as good at bending his style to suit the prevailing wind as he was at composing the music in the first place.

+ AT A GLANCE +

THOMAS TALLIS
BORN: AROUND 1505
DIED: 1585
NATIONALITY: ENGLISH
MUST LISTEN: *SPEM IN ALIUM*

Tallis's exact provenance has been lost in the mists of time, but he was probably brought up near Canterbury, working first as an organist at Dover Priory. He then moved to Waltham Abbey in Essex in the same role, before becoming a lay clerk at Canterbury Cathedral.

From 1543 until his death more than four decades later, Tallis operated a job share with his pupil **William Byrd** as the composer and organist to the Chapel Royal.

+ AT A GLANCE +

WILLIAM BYRD
BORN: AROUND 1540
DIED: 1623
NATIONALITY: ENGLISH
MUST LISTEN: *AVE VERUM CORPUS*

William Byrd was known as 'the father of British music'. The fact that he survived to write anything at all is surprising, considering that he was known to be a Catholic supporter at a time when this was punishable by death. He became organist and choirmaster at Lincoln Cathedral in 1563, where he stayed until 1572 when he moved to London to take up the job share with Thomas Tallis.

Whereas Tallis wrote only a few pieces that were not for the Church, Byrd left behind some excellent examples of keyboard music and of madrigals. (Madrigals are unaccompanied songs for a group of voices.)

Byrd and Tallis lived out their lives in relative financial comfort because of the beneficence of Elizabeth I. She granted them jointly a patent that allowed them a complete monopoly on printing music and music paper in England for 21 years from 1575. Their first publication was called *Cantiones Sacrae*, which translates as 'Sacred Songs'. It was made up of a total of 34 different songs – 17 by each composer.

This new means of distributing music meant that, for the first time, choirs could sing music from printed sheets, making it far easier for musical works to become established right across the country.

Back to Italy now, and it is important to remember that innovation in sacred music was not necessarily welcomed with open arms by the Catholic Church. Some of the changes were even the subject of papal decrees. With the rise of Protestantism, any modification of the status quo tended to be regarded as an all-out attack on the foundations of the Church itself. Some senior members of the Church even advocated changing things back to the style written by composers of the likes of Hildegard of Bingen, because they believed that the fancy new way of writing music meant that the sacred texts no longer had the same powerful meaning.

***

+ AT A GLANCE +

GIOVANNI PIERLUIGI DA PALESTRINA
BORN: AROUND 1525
DIED: 1594
NATIONALITY: ITALIAN
MUST LISTEN: *MISSA PAPAE MARCELLI*

***

Giovanni Pierluigi da Palestrina was asked to compose a Mass that would definitively prove one way or another whether polyphony really was the way forward for Church music, rather than the plainsong of old.

Palestrina produced a Mass that was so beautiful that the critics gave up and the polyphonic brigade was victorious. He dedicated this new piece, which was composed around 1561, to Pope Marcellus.

The Pope reigned for only 55 days and never actually heard the music that was written especially for him.

Palestrina had some particularly unhappy periods during his life. In the 1570s, his family was torn apart by the plague, which was sweeping through Europe with devastating consequences. His wife, brother and two of his sons all succumbed to the terrible disease.

We now stay in Italy for the rest of this period of classical music. As you will see as the historical part of our book continues, there were strong English, French, Austrian, German, Russian and Eastern European influences on classical music at various times in its history. Italy could argue the case for being the most influential country of all – and nowhere has that Italian influence been more keenly felt than in the world of opera.

Opera was a really major development in classical music. In its most basic form, opera marks the coming together of words and music in an equal partnership.

+ AT A GLANCE +

JACOPO PERI
BORN: 1561
DIED: 1633
NATIONALITY: ITALIAN
MUST LISTEN: THE OLDEST REMAINING
OPERA *EURIDICE*

The man to whom history has given credit for writing the world's first opera is one **Jacopo Peri**, whose first operatic work was *Dafne*. The composer himself was something of a performer and he took the role of Apollo in the first production in 1598. Although we know the opera performance took place, the music has now been lost. However, Peri's second opera, *Euridice*, does still exist and is occasionally performed today.

Although he has no right to claim the title at all, many people consider **Claudio Monteverdi's** *La Favola d'Orfeo* to be the first true opera. It's based on the same story as *Euridice*. Orpheus (Orfeo) and Euridice are husband and wife in the mythological tale. The story goes that Orpheus was so distraught at Euridice's death that he visited Hades, the land of the dead, to try to get her back. He ultimately fails in his quest. It was a story to which other composers returned time and time again during later periods of classical music.

✦ AT A GLANCE ✦

CLAUDIO MONTEVERDI
BORN: 1567
DIED: 1643
NATIONALITY: ITALIAN
MUST LISTEN: *VESPERS FOR THE BLESSED VIRGIN*

Monteverdi is also known today for his sacred music, and in particular for his *Vespers for the Blessed Virgin*, dedicated to Pope Paul V. This is a strikingly beautiful piece of music, which was written shortly after both Monteverdi's wife and his only child had died. It is quite likely that his own personal suffering is mirrored in the music.

THE END OF EARLY MUSIC

The advent of opera marks the end of the longest period of music in *Everything You Ever Wanted To Know About Classical Music ... but were too afraid to ask*. It began at the dawn of time, or around the year 1000, depending on your point of view, and ended at around the turn of the 17th century.

It is worth noting at this point that the beginning and end of each musical era cannot be pinpointed to an absolute moment in time. One set of composers did not simply stop writing, to be replaced by a new team waiting patiently on the subs' bench. Instead, new styles of music gradually replaced old styles – just as plainsong gave way to polyphony and Medieval composers were replaced by Renaissance composers, so they in turn faded away. You will be relieved to know that our story most certainly doesn't end there, though.

CHAPTER 5

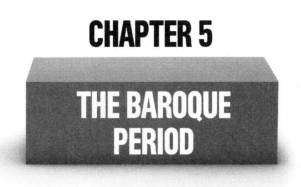

THE BAROQUE PERIOD

BAROQUE 'N' ROLL

Had this book been written by an American, the heading above would probably have been 'If it ain't baroque, don't fix it', because our cousins across the Atlantic pronounce the word 'Baroque' with a long 'o', so the second syllable rhymes with 'poke'. But back here in Britain, we always pronounce it with a short 'o', to rhyme with 'clock'.

WHAT ELSE WAS GOING ON IN THE WORLD?

Anyway, enough of the pronunciation guide. We are now in the period of classical music that runs from 1600 to 1750. This was a rather exciting time in history, with plenty of storylines for action movies: Guy Fawkes attempted to blow up the Houses of Parliament in the Gunpowder Plot; the Pilgrim Fathers set sail on the *Mayflower* from Plymouth for a new life in America; and Charles I was beheaded. It was also a period of enormous scientific advancement: Isaac Newton realized that the earth had a gravitational pull, so the story goes, after being hit on the head by an apple, and astronomers also decided once and for all that the earth orbits the sun, rather than vice versa.

FROM CHURCH TO NOBILITY

The Church was still an important force in deciding what music would be written, not least because it employed so many composers in a variety of musical positions. However, as the story of the Baroque period unfurls, you will begin to notice a shift in power. Gradually, the Church becomes a less important force in the commissioning of new music, to be replaced by the nobility, who listened to music chiefly for recreational pleasure rather than out of devotional duty, and who commissioned composers and employed musicians as a means of showing off their status within society.

We begin our journey through the Baroque composers with two men who are firmly in the sacred music camp.

✦ AT A GLANCE ✦

GREGORIO ALLEGRI
BORN: 1582
DIED: 1652
NATIONALITY: ITALIAN
MUST LISTEN: *MISERERE*

Gregorio Allegri was steeped in the traditions of the Catholic Church, becoming a choirboy at the age of nine and ending up as music director of the papal choir two years before his death.

He is best known today for his *Miserere*, which was performed every year during Holy Week from the time it was written until towards the end of the 19th century. The Vatican kept the lid on the exact details of what was being sung, and anyone who made an illegal copy of the music was threatened with severe punishment. The *Miserere* was probably even more stunning to listen to back in Allegri's time than it is today because the members of the highly skilled papal choir would add their own embellishments to the music – an example of 17th-century choral jamming, if you like. This piece of music also warrants a mention during the life of one Wolfgang Amadeus Mozart later on in Chapter 6 of this book.

The English composer **Orlando Gibbons** was a member of the Chapel Royal. This choir still exists today and is an important part of the royal household's music-making. You will often see the choir performing at state occasions. The Chapel Royal was something of a hothouse for the best musical talent in England and, because it was the monarch's own choir, it was able to cherry-pick the very best musicians from all of the other choirs around the country. As well as Orlando Gibbons, Thomas Tallis, William Byrd and Henry Purcell were all important members of this august body.

Gibbons was a particularly talented organist, and he also wrote keyboard works and pieces to be performed by consorts (groups of musicians). It is worth noting that Gibbons was the first major composer to write exclusively for the Anglican Church. He died tragically young while with the royal household in Canterbury, where he is buried in the cathedral.

Jean-Baptiste Lully held a privileged position in the French court, working as the personal composer to King Louis XIV. His job made him the most important man in French music, and for more than two decades he was able to exert enormous control over the country's musical life.

During this time, Lully achieved a lot, particularly in developing the sound of the orchestra. After his changes, orchestras looked and sounded far closer to the ones we have today than they did to those that had pre-dated him.

Lully was undoubtedly an innovator and a visionary. Many of the instruments that he brought into the orchestra had only just been invented, so, although an orchestra made up of 24 violins plus flutes, oboes, bassoons, trumpets and timpani might seem normal to us, it was absolutely revolutionary in the 1600s.

Lully also bought the right to be the only man in France to be allowed to put on operas – he staged his first production on a converted tennis court. He was also extremely influential in the area of music publishing and became well known for writing ballets.

Lully's death was the stuff of legend. Rather than the conductor's baton that we know today, Lully used a long stick to beat time on the floor when he was conducting his orchestra. One day, he missed the floor and speared his own foot instead. Gangrene set in and he died two months later after refusing to have his foot amputated. His royal patronage did, however, ensure that he died an extremely rich man.

+ AT A GLANCE +

MARC-ANTOINE CHARPENTIER
BORN: 1643
DIED: 1704
NATIONALITY: FRENCH
MUST LISTEN: *TE DEUM*

Although he lived at the same time as Lully, **Marc-Antoine Charpentier** was never part of Louis XIV's court. His choral music has come back into fashion in recent years, but his best-known work is infamous for an altogether different reason.

Next time you settle down in front of the television to watch the *Eurovision Song Contest*, listen to the opening theme music: it is the trumpet tune at the very start of Charpentier's *Te Deum*. You can rest assured that it will be just about the only piece of music that you hear all evening that doesn't deserve 'nul points'.

+ AT A GLANCE +

ARCANGELO CORELLI
BORN: 1653
DIED: 1713
NATIONALITY: ITALIAN
MUST LISTEN: *CONCERTO GROSSO, OP. 6 NO. 8,*
KNOWN AS *'THE CHRISTMAS CONCERTO*

Arcangelo Corelli was born into a rich family and was lucky enough not to face the hand-to-mouth financial struggles that many other composers were forced to endure. Despite what some of the self-appointed grandees of the classical music world would have you believe, most composers tended to write music as a means of putting food on their tables, a roof over their heads and clothes on their backs, and not because of some sort of flight of artistic fancy.

Perhaps it was Corelli's relative wealth that made him less hungry to produce a copious amount of work or perhaps because he didn't need to keep an eye on the money coming in he could spend more time refining his music but he was by no means the most prolific composer of his time. He was, however, celebrated across Europe, and many of the greatest composers who followed him, such as Bach and Handel, were undoubtedly influenced by the music he wrote.

Corelli was an outstanding violin player, and he is the first of our featured composers to make a name purely from the composition of instrumental music. He also brought some new thinking to the way that orchestras performed, insisting that all the string players mirrored each other's playing style by moving their bows up and down in the same direction at the same time. Believe it or not, this actually changed the sound made by the orchestra, allowing the musicians to give a more precise performance. It also made Corelli's orchestras visually far more aesthetically pleasing, and his concerts became popular because they were as easy on the eye as they were on the ear.

Corelli was also the master of the concerto grosso, a type of musical work where the orchestra is divided into two different groups. One group of musicians tended to play first, with a second group then echoing the music played by the first set. This created a sense of drama between the louder and quieter parts of the music and between the two groups of players.

✦ AT A GLANCE ✦

JOHANN PACHELBEL
BORN: 1653
DIED: 1706
NATIONALITY: GERMAN
MUST LISTEN: *CANON IN D*

At Classic FM, we have a term for those composers who are known for one great work that dwarfs all the rest of their output. We call them 'one-hit wonders'. The German **Johann Pachelbel** is a prime example of the species, with his *Canon in D* a firm favourite in all sorts of environments, not least as an accompaniment to the walk down the aisle at many weddings.

Many composers wrote canons – but nobody else achieved quite the same fame for it. It's a simple idea in which a melody is played and then imitated by one or more other instruments. You may unwittingly have performed a canon yourself as a child when you sang 'Frère Jacques', 'Three Blind Mice' or 'London's Burning'. In these cases, the canon is sometimes referred to as a 'round'.

Although the *Canon in D* is pretty much all he is remembered for now, Pachelbel was massive in the world of keyboard and chamber music in the late 17th century. (Just to remind you from our earlier section on musical terms, any piece that is written for small groups of musicians to play counts as chamber music. We even have chamber orchestras, which are smaller than symphony orchestras and often feature up to around 30 players.)

✦ AT A GLANCE ✦

HENRY PURCELL
BORN: 1659
DIED: 1695
NATIONALITY: ENGLISH
MUST LISTEN: 'WHEN I AM LAID IN EARTH' (KNOWN AS 'DIDO'S
LAMENT'); THE 'RONDO' FROM ABDELAZAR; TRUMPET
TUNE AND AIR IN D; 'COME YE SONS OF ART'

This book is filled to the brim with musical prodigies and **Henry Purcell** is the first of them. It is just as well that his talent was identified and nurtured while he was young, because he was just 36 years old when he died – although he achieved more than many composers who lived to be twice his age. Music historians say that his death was a real setback for the development of English music. It was not for another 200 years that England would produce another truly great composer, in the shape of Edward Elgar.

By the time Purcell was ten, he was one of the Children of the Chapel Royal (a choirboy). Just a decade later, he was given one of the most prestigious musical jobs of the moment when he was made organist of Westminster Abbey.

Purcell produced a large amount of music, considering his short life, and its range was wide – taking in organ solos, sacred anthems, secular songs, chamber music and music to be performed in the theatre. He wrote works for Charles II, James II and Queen Mary.

Purcell's only opera, *Dido and Aeneas*, tells the story of Dido, the Queen of Carthage. She is in love with Aeneas, who sails away to found Rome. She is devastated and sings the haunting aria 'When I Am Laid in Earth' – in our opinion the greatest thing Purcell ever wrote.

Our next composer is most famous for a piece of music that he never actually completed (and quite possibly didn't actually write at all). The music today that we regard as being **Tomaso Albinoni's** *Adagio in G minor* was (it's claimed) based on only a fragment of manuscript, rather than a fully realised work. This fragment was taken by an Italian professor, Remo Giazotto, who built it up into the piece we know and love today, based on his studies of the composer's other works. It would be fair to say that Giazotto took an informed guess as to how Albinoni intended the *Adagio* to turn out.

+ AT A GLANCE +

TOMASO GIOVANNI ALBINONI
BORN: 1671
DIED: 1750
NATIONALITY: ITALIAN
MUST LISTEN: *ADAGIO IN G MINOR*
(SEE CAVEAT BELOW); *OBOE CONCERTO,
OP. 9 NO. 2*

It's hard not to feel just a little sorry for Albinoni because there are plenty of other surviving pieces that he definitely did write, for which he could be remembered. The 300 or so works to his name include more than 50 operas and more than 50 concertos.

Antonio Vivaldi was responsible for what many people reckon is the most recorded piece of classical music of all time: the *Four Seasons*. Every year, new versions are released, but for our money, it's hard to beat the 1989 version by Nigel Kennedy on the EMI Classics label.

+ AT A GLANCE +

ANTONIO VIVALDI
BORN: 1678
DIED: 1741
NATIONALITY: ITALIAN
MUST LISTEN: *FOUR SEASONS*; *GLORIA*; 'NULLA IN
MUNDO PAX SINCERA', WHICH WAS
USED IN THE FILM *SHINE*

It's all the more remarkable that this work has achieved the success it has when you consider that Vivaldi's music was hardly played at all from his death in 1741 through until the middle of the 20th century. This is all down to a rather strange decision by a nobleman called Count Giacomo Durazzo. He pulled together all of Vivaldi's original works and simply locked them up. In his last will and testament, Durazzo ordered his family to make sure that none of this music by Vivaldi should ever be performed or published. After many years, these ludicrous instructions were overturned and Vivaldi's music was once more heard. The public lapped up his catchy melodies, and a star was reborn, some 200 years after his death.

Vivaldi certainly rattled out the concertos, with more than 500 of them to his name. Unkind critics suggest that he actually wrote the same tune in a slightly different way 500 times, but we don't think that's entirely fair.

There is no doubt that Vivaldi was a bit of a character. He chose to follow in his father's footsteps and learned to play the violin. He played the instrument while undertaking his religious training, becoming known as 'The Red Priest' because of his bright red hair.

Vivaldi was excused having to say Mass because he claimed to suffer from asthma. This illness certainly didn't stop him from conducting or from travelling all over Europe. It also didn't prevent him from enjoying a close relationship with at least one of his travelling companions, a young soprano called Anna Girò and quite possibly with her sister Paolina as well. He was censured for unpriestly conduct in 1737, despite denying that his relationship with the two women was in any way improper.

Any illicit affairs certainly never got in the way of Vivaldi's composing, though. As well as the 500 concertos, he also wrote more than 50 operas, well over 80 sonatas and more than 120 other sacred and secular vocal pieces.

Vivaldi was a mere minnow in terms of productivity when compared to our next composer. In the race to write the largest number of pieces **Georg Philipp Telemann** is not only miles ahead of the rest of the Baroque pack, he storms in front of every other composer that we have featured so far – or in the pages still to come – with around 3,700 different works to his name.

+ **AT A GLANCE** +

GEORG PHILIPP TELEMANN
BORN: 1681
DIED: 1767
NATIONALITY: GERMAN
MUST LISTEN: *CONCERTO IN D FOR TRUMPET AND STRINGS*

Telemann had a keen ear for the prevailing musical fashions and he also made sure that his pieces were heard far and wide. He was one of the first composers to publish his vocal and instrumental music in a magazine format specifically targeted at amateur music-makers.

Although he was considered to be a real star in Germany during his lifetime, history has not judged Telemann so kindly, and his musical contribution has been completely eclipsed by that of our next two composers – the undoubted kings of the Baroque period.

+ **AT A GLANCE** +

JOHANN SEBASTIAN BACH
BORN: 1685
DIED: 1750
NATIONALITY: GERMAN
MUST LISTEN: *BRANDENBURG CONCERTOS; TOCCATA AND FUGUE IN D MINOR; ST MATTHEW PASSION; GOLDBERG VARIATIONS*

George Frideric Handel and **Johann Sebastian Bach** were born in Germany in the same year: 1685 was a very fine musical vintage indeed.

Johann Sebastian Bach had music in his blood. He was part of a German musical dynasty that spanned many generations, both before and after him. Some people believe that his music actually eclipses that of those two other giants of the classical music world – Mozart and Beethoven. Whatever the ranking, there is no doubt that Bach deserves to be among those considered as the greatest ever classical composers.

After he had died, there was a general reassessment of just how good a composer Bach really was and he gained the recognition that he deserved as a master of musical composition, particularly in the areas of choral, keyboard and instrumental works. There is a particularly strong spirituality to his music, which was influenced by Bach's dedicated religious faith.

By the time Johann Sebastian had reached double figures in age, both his parents had died. The young boy was sent to live with his older brother, Johann Christoph, who was, like their father, an organist.

Johann Christoph passed his skills on the organ to his younger brother. When Johann Sebastian was 15, he went away to a school 200 miles away and continued to study for another two years.

After leaving school, Johann Sebastian worked as a violinist before eventually taking up the family business and becoming an organist. One of the best-known stories about Bach concerns the lengths to which he would go to learn more about making music. On one occasion, when he was just 19, he made a 450-mile round trip on foot to hear a concert by his hero, the organist Dietrich Buxtehude.

In 1707, Bach married his cousin, Maria Barbara Bach. His first big job came a year later when he was appointed organist to the Duke of Saxe-Weimar. He stayed in the job for nine years, although his relationship with his boss became more than a little rocky towards the end of tenure, when he asked to leave for another job after being passed over for promotion. The Duke became so fed up with him that Bach was thrown in jail for a month. It wasn't the first time that Bach had fallen out with his employers; he had upset the Church authorities in one of his previous roles. He was definitely one of those people who reacted very badly to being told what to do.

In the end, Bach got his way and left to join the court of Prince Leopold of Anhalt-Cöthen as 'Kapellmeister' – the modern equivalent would be 'Director of Music'. Bach wrote much of his instrumental and orchestral music here. In 1720, his wife Maria died, but it didn't take Bach long to find a replacement, and his wedding to Anna Magdalena Wilcken took place just a year later.

In total, Bach had 20 children, although because of the high infant mortality rates at the time, only nine survived beyond their early childhood. Of these, Wilhelm Friedemann, Carl Philipp Emanuel,

Johann Christoph Friedrich and Johann Christian all became composers.

Bach moved on to a job at a school in Leipzig in 1723, where he spent the final 27 years of his life. It might come as a surprise now, but Bach was in fact the second choice for the job, with Telemann being offered it first. As well as teaching, Bach was organist and choirmaster in the local church. He was required to create a huge number of choral pieces, and it was hard work. Once again, Bach fell out with the authorities, although this time he opted to stick with the job until the bitter end.

Among the many wonderful pieces Bach wrote during this period of his life, the two Easter works – the *St John Passion* and the *St Matthew Passion* – particularly stand out. On a more light-hearted note, he also wrote 'The Coffee Cantata' for a music group that met in a local coffee house.

Bach always had a strong interest in maths and liked to represent numbers in his music. He believed that 14 was his own personal number because that was the total of his name scored when he added up the alphabetical position of each of its component letters. Patterns around the number 14 often appear in his music.

Towards the end of his life, Bach suffered from cataracts, and his eyesight began to fail. The English surgeon John Taylor botched an operation to cure the problem, just as he had done with Handel, and Bach was left almost totally blind. Just before Bach died something happened that corrected the problems with his eyes naturally, and for a short period he was able to see well enough to continue working on his final piece, *The Art of Fugue*.

Bach's rate of composition was quite remarkable, and after he died it took no fewer than 46 years to collect and publish all his works.

Handel's father was not at all keen on his son taking up music as a career, and he banned the young boy from having anything to do with it, preferring him to study law before ending up with a sensible, secure job. Handel's mother, on the other hand, seemed to recognise talent when she heard it. History has it that she smuggled a small harpsichord into the attic of their home, where George Frideric would practise away, out of his father's earshot.

When Handel was eight years old, the Duke of Saxe-Weissenfels heard him play. The Duke was so impressed that he ensured that the boy had lessons. Such was Handel's natural talent that just three years later his tutor said that there was nothing left that he could teach him. Remarkably, this appears to have been the last time that Handel had formal music tuition; he was 11.

+ AT A GLANCE +

GEORGE FRIDERIC HANDEL
BORN: 1685
DIED: 1759
NATIONALITY: INITIALLY GERMAN AND THEN ENGLISH
MUST LISTEN: *MESSIAH*; *'OMBRA MAI FU'* FROM THE OPERA
XERXES; *'ZADOK THE PRIEST'* (USED IN THE FILM *THE MADNESS
OF KING GEORGE* AND ALSO THE VERY FIRST PIECE OF MUSIC
THAT WE EVER PLAYED ON CLASSIC FM, ON 7 SEPTEMBER 1992);
WATER MUSIC; *'ARRIVAL OF THE QUEEN OF SHEBA'*
FROM THE ORATORIO *SOLOMON*.

In his late teens, Handel took up a role as an organist before moving to Hamburg, where he tried his hand at writing opera. He decided to move to Italy in order to improve that particular skill.

After around four years soaking up as much of the Italian music scene as he possibly could, Handel travelled to Hanover, where he was given a position in the court of the Elector.

The travel bug had well and truly bitten, though, and Handel asked for permission to visit England. His request was granted and he set off across the English Channel. Handel was a big hit in London, and his opera *Rinaldo* was greeted with universal acclaim – even though he had written it in just 15 days. Although he did eventually return to Germany, Handel later travelled again to London, where he repeated his initial success.

By now, Handel was really pushing his luck as far as his employer was concerned. He was still on the payroll in Hanover, yet spent all his time away from the court. Suddenly, everything changed for him – and it was a change for the better.

The English monarch, Queen Anne, died. The heir to the throne was

Handel's boss, the Elector of Hanover, who became King George I. The new King forgave Handel's absence, employing him in London. Handel must have felt at home in the city because this was the period when he wrote many of his greatest works, including his *Water Music*, which he composed in 1717 for a royal pageant on the River Thames.

In 1727, George I died and Handel continued to compose for George II, with 'Zadok the Priest' written as a Coronation anthem. It has been sung at the Coronation of every British monarch ever since.

Handel's *Music for the Royal Fireworks* was composed for a display put on by King George II in London's Hyde Park. The music was a triumph, but the fireworks were an unmitigated disaster, with one particular catherine wheel setting fire to a wooden tower and causing pandemonium in the crowd.

One of Handel's most performed works today is his oratorio *Messiah*. It was written in aid of three Irish charities and was given its premiere in Dublin in 1741. It includes the incredibly uplifting 'Hallelujah Chorus', which is today heard regularly at Christmas and Easter. It was another example of how speedily Handel could produce the goods when required: even though the music lasts for two and a half hours, *Messiah* took him just 24 days to write.

Handel created the most incredible music and was undoubtedly a complex character. He was grumpy, speaking English with a heavy accent and muttering constantly to himself in German; he had atrocious table manners and was a greedy eater.

Handel's success is a fine example of classical music's ability to cross geographical divides. Here was a man who was born in Germany yet became one of English music's greatest success stories, still being seen as part of the English Establishment centuries after his death. If you ever visit Westminster Abbey, make sure you pause to pay tribute to Handel: his body still lies there today.

When you talk about Scarlatti, make sure you refer to the right one. We're focusing on **Domenico Scarlatti**, rather than his lesser-known father, Alessandro.

Scarlatti was by no means as great a composer as the previous two giants of the Baroque period, with whom he shared the same birth year. He was, however, a fine keyboard player, and much of his best work was for the keyboard. Scarlatti wrote 500 or so sonatas for the instrument.

+ AT A GLANCE +

DOMENICO SCARLATTI
BORN: 1685
DIED: 1757
NATIONALITY: ITALIAN
MUST LISTEN: *SONATA IN A, KK 182*

Legend suggests that Scarlatti once had a keyboard duel with Handel. The former played the harpsichord and the latter the organ. The judges appear to have sat on the fence when it came to naming the winner: Scarlatti was declared the better harpsichordist and Handel the better organist.

+ AT A GLANCE +

DOMENICO ZIPOLI
BORN: 1688
DIED: 1726
NATIONALITY: ITALIAN
MUST LISTEN: *ELEVAZIONE*

Our final composer from the Baroque period is one of the least well documented. He became more famous in South America than he ever did in his native Italy. **Domenico Zipoli** was born in Naples, but towards the end of his life he emigrated to Argentina. His *Elevazione* has become a big favourite of Classic FM listeners. Two hundred years after his death, new repertoire by Zipoli was still being discovered. In the 1970s, around 20 previously unknown works turned up in Bolivia; he must have composed them while serving as a Jesuit missionary in Paraguay.

THE END OF THE BAROQUE PERIOD

Appropriately enough, Zipoli brings to an end our A-to-Z of composers from the Baroque period, which began back at the turn of the 17th century with Allegri. The Baroque composers marked 150 years of musical development. The influence of the Church at the end of the Baroque period was far less marked than it was at the end of the Early Music period. Kings, queens and noblemen were now major forces in commissioning new music and employing musicians to perform it. This was the period when classical music became showbiz – even though showbiz wouldn't be invented for another couple of hundred years.

There were, however, still a huge number of changes to come during the next period of classical music – a time that many people regard as being at the very heart of the whole genre.

CHAPTER 6

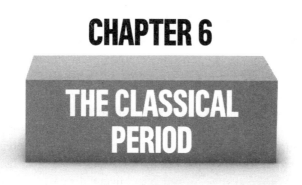

THE CLASSICAL PERIOD

ISN'T IT ALL CLASSICAL?

Just in case you skipped the introductory pages of this book, this is a reminder that although everything we play on Classic FM is classical music, there was also a Classical period of classical music. It was neatly sandwiched between the Baroque period that we have just lived through, and the Romantic period, which is still to come. Broadly speaking, the Classical period runs from 1750 until 1830, so it is actually the shortest of all the periods that we cover.

Don't for a moment think that because this particular period spanned only eight decades, it was in any way light on new developments, big names or stunning music. As you will see, it has all three by the bucket-load.

As well as embracing the three classical greats – Haydn, Mozart and Beethoven – the Classical period also saw the development of the classical symphony and concerto into the form that we would regard as being normal today. More and more, composers were also being thought of as stars in their own right, as classical music became a far wider pursuit among the middle classes.

WHAT ELSE WAS GOING ON IN THE WORLD?

Scientific invention continued apace and the Industrial Revolution arrived in Britain. Steam was harnessed for the first time as a means of powering large-scale factory production. James Hargreaves came up with the 'Spinning Jenny', which revolutionised the cotton industry, and Benjamin Franklin invented the lightning conductor.

Big strides were made in the world of transport: James Brindley designed the Worsley-to-Manchester Canal; the first railway opened from Stockton to Darlington; and man flew for the very first time when two French brothers, Joseph and Jacques Montgolfier, created the first hot-air balloon in 1783.

James Cook discovered Australia and, not long afterwards, the first convicts started being shipped out. Meanwhile, America gained its independence and France underwent a revolution, which resulted in it losing its monarchy.

OUR CLASSICAL TOP TEN

In this chapter, we will be concentrating on ten composers from the Classical period – some extremely well known, others less so. Yet all influenced the development of the Classical period of classical music.

+ AT A GLANCE +

CHRISTOPH WILLIBALD VON GLUCK
BORN: 1714
DIED: 1787
NATIONALITY: GERMAN
MUST LISTEN: *ORPHEUS AND EURIDICE*

It is for his contribution to the opera world that **Christoph Willibald von Gluck** is best remembered today. Just as Purcell and Monteverdi had done before, Gluck took the story of Orpheus and Euridice and turned it into an opera. His style was very different from that of previous composers, with a greater emphasis on characterisation and story-telling. He also included two sections of ballet in the opera, including *The Dance of the Blessed Spirits*, which remains very popular today.

Gluck cleaned opera up from being a vehicle for star singers to show off to one that allowed the story to shine through. He was among the first composers to use clarinets, cor anglaises (they look like over-sized oboes) and trombones in his operas.

Gluck died in Vienna after suffering a series of strokes. It is believed that his death was brought on by his insistence on drinking an after-dinner liqueur, even though his doctor had forbidden him to do so.

+ AT A GLANCE +

CARL PHILIPP EMANUEL BACH
BORN: 1714
DIED: 1788
NATIONALITY: GERMAN
MUST LISTEN: *HARPSICHORD CONCERTO IN
D MINOR*; *MAGNIFICAT*

Carl Philipp Emanuel Bach was born in the same year as Gluck. You would, of course, be right in thinking that the name sounds familiar. Carl Philipp Emanuel Bach was the son of Johann Sebastian Bach. Although he was nowhere near as important a composer as his father, Carl Philipp Emanuel did make a significant contribution to the development of the Classical sound, acting as a bridge between the Baroque style encapsulated by Johann Sebastian and the clearly different Classical style of composers such as Haydn and Mozart – of whom, more in a moment. Carl Philipp Emanuel's earliest works sounded very much like those of his father, whereas his later works were more similar to Haydn's.

During his lifetime, Carl Philipp Emanuel was famous as a keyboard player, working for King Frederick the Great for some 28 years. As a composer, he developed the sound of the sonata. He took over from Telemann as music director in Hamburg, where he was in charge of around 200 performances a year in five different churches. Carl Philipp Emanuel managed to find time to write a manual called *The Art of Keyboard Playing*, which was used by many of the pianists who followed him. As his name is such a mouthful, you'll also hear him referred to as C. P. E. Bach.

+ AT A GLANCE +

JOSEPH HAYDN
BORN: 1732
DIED: 1809
NATIONALITY: AUSTRIAN
MUST LISTEN: *THE CREATION*;
SYMPHONY NO. 101 ('CLOCK'); *CELLO
CONCERTOS NOS. 1 AND 2*; *THE SEASONS*

Joseph Haydn was one of the great architects of the Classical period of classical music. He lived longer than many of his contemporaries and witnessed huge developments in the way that music was written during his 77-year life. Haydn was particularly influential in developing the symphony, sonata and string quartet, and was to become a major inspiration to those who followed him, including Mozart and Beethoven.

Haydn was another man with a tremendous creative urge, publishing around 1,200 works, including no fewer than 104 symphonies, more than 80 string quartets, over 50 piano sonatas, at least 24 concertos and 20 operas. Then there are nearly 90 choral works, more than 100 songs, plus literally hundreds of other pieces for solo instruments or chamber groups, all of which bore Haydn's name.

Back in Haydn's day, castrati were still relatively common. These were men, who, without putting too fine a point on it, had been operated on to ensure that their voices never actually broke. Haydn had a magnificent singing voice as a boy and his choirmaster suggested he could keep it for ever if he would just undergo a very small operation. Haydn was happy to go along with the idea, until his horrified father found out what was about to happen and the boy was told what the operation would actually entail.

Haydn was able to compose so much principally because of the patronage of the Esterházy family, who were extremely influential within Hungarian society. He also became one of the first truly international musical figures, making tours around Europe, in the way that Take That or Coldplay might do today. Haydn was particularly popular on his visits to England, and he had two long stays in the country at the end of his life. This allowed him to build up quite a treasure chest of riches – he was most certainly not the stereotypical impoverished composer we shall meet so often in *Everything You Ever Wanted To Know About Classical Music ... but were too afraid to ask.*

Haydn's success is all the more remarkable because he appears, in the main, to have taught himself about music. This seems to have been a benefit rather than a drawback, allowing him to develop his own style of composing, free from the constraints of the perceived wisdoms of the time.

It is for his symphonies that Haydn is most remembered today. Many of them were given nicknames, with fun stories attached as to how they got those names.

Take the *'Farewell' Symphony No. 45*, for example. This was composed while Haydn was working for the Esterházy family. The court musicians were fed up with being separated from their wives and families. Haydn wanted to get the message across to his boss, so the musical score instructed the musicians one by one to blow out the candles by their music stands and exit the stage. At the end, only the two principal violinists are left.

The nicknames go on, including the *'Clock' Symphony No. 101*, so called because of the tick-tocking slow movement, and the *'Surprise' Symphony No. 94*, with its deafening chord that comes crashing in after a very quiet opening. There are many others too: *'Philosopher'*, *'Mercury'*, *'Schoolmaster'*, *'Bear'*, *'Hen'*, *'Miracle'*, and a whole group known as the *'London Symphonies'*.

+ AT A GLANCE +

JOHANN CHRISTIAN BACH
BORN: 1735
DIED: 1782
NATIONALITY: GERMAN
MUST LISTEN: *SYMPHONIES, OP. 3*, WHICH IS ACTUALLY MADE UP OF SIX WORKS

During his lifetime, **Johann Christian Bach** was far more famous than his father, Johann Sebastian Bach, had been in his. Johann Christian's claim to fame was that he was the first person to give a solo piano performance in London, and he is sometimes referred to as 'The London Bach'.

Johann Christian made a lot of money early on in his career, but things went wrong for him financially towards the end of his life and his reputation started to wane.

+ **AT A GLANCE** +

KARL DITTERS VON DITTERSDORF
BORN: 1739
DIED: 1799
NATIONALITY: AUSTRIAN
MUST LISTEN: *HARP CONCERTO*

Karl Ditters von Dittersdorf does not appear in this book because he was by any means the most influential or creative composer of the Classical period. In fact, many histories of classical music don't include him at all. He is here as an act of self-indulgence because of his wonderful name, which has been a great favourite with Classic FM presenters over the years.

Now largely forgotten, Dittersdorf was actually one of the most popular composers in Europe during his lifetime, although he never managed to turn that popularity into financial stability. He wrote more than 120 symphonies and 45 operas, as well as choral and chamber

---

+ **AT A GLANCE** +

LUIGI BOCCHERINI
BORN: 1743
DIED: 1805
NATIONALITY: ITALIAN
MUST LISTEN: *STRING QUINTET IN E;*
CELLO CONCERTO NO. 9

---

works. His music deserves to have a wider hearing and, with a name like that, he might just catch the public's imagination once again.

He might have written around 600 different works, but **Luigi Boccherini** is famous today for just one piece – the *'Minuet'* from his *String Quintet in E*, which featured in the British cinema classic *The Ladykillers*, as mentioned earlier. Boccherini actually wrote 154 different quintets for various combinations of instruments.

During his lifetime, Boccherini was a star performer on the cello, touring Italy, France and Spain. His life ended unhappily, though. He outlived his two wives and several of his children and was himself unwell for some years, before eventually dying in poverty. Had he lived just a few years longer, Boccherini would have seen his music coming back into fashion.

✦ AT A GLANCE ✦

ANTONIO SALIERI
BORN: 1750
DIED: 1825
NATIONALITY: ITALIAN
MUST LISTEN: *FLUTE AND OBOE CONCERTO*

Our next composer is famous today for a crime he did not commit rather than for the music he wrote. However, for more than five decades, **Antonio Salieri** was one of the most influential forces in the Viennese musical world. He enjoyed great success as an opera composer in Italy and France. Towards the end of his life, he concentrated on teaching.

Depending on your point of view, Salieri was either done a great disservice, or his place in history was secured by Pushkin's 1831 play *Mozart and Salieri* and Peter Schaffer's stunning 1979 play *Amadeus*, which became an equally stunning 1984 film of the same name.

To find out why, we need look no further than our very next composer.

+ AT A GLANCE +

WOLFGANG AMADEUS MOZART
BORN: 1756
DIED: 1791
NATIONALITY: AUSTRIAN
MUST LISTEN: 'LAUDATE DOMINUM'; REQUIEM; CLARINET
CONCERTO; PIANO CONCERTO NO. 21; HORN CONCERTO NO. 4;
SERENADE NO. 13 ('EINE KLEINE NACHTMUSIK'); SYMPHONY
NO. 41 ('JUPITER'); COSÌ FAN TUTTE; DON GIOVANNI;
THE MAGIC FLUTE; THE MARRIAGE OF FIGARO

The argument rages between Mozart and Beethoven fans: which one was truly the greatest? The composer who appears to be in the ascendant at any given moment tends to depend on who has celebrated a significant anniversary most recently. If we look to the Classic FM Hall of Fame for help, then we find that Mozart consistently has more entries in the Top 300 than Beethoven, but a greater number of Beethoven's works tend to be clustered more towards the higher echelons of the chart. So with honours fairly even between the two, there is little doubt in our minds at Classic FM that, along with Johann Sebastian Bach, Mozart and Beethoven are the true giants of classical music composition.

Johannes Chrysostomus Wolfgangus Amadeus Mozart was born in Salzburg on a snowy evening in January 1756. He was an incredible child prodigy, playing the piano at the age of three and composing by the time he was just four years old.

His father Leopold was a composer and musician who worked for the Prince Archbishop of Salzburg. His talent was nowhere near as great as that of his son, but music appears to have been in the Mozart family's blood, and Wolfgang's sister, Maria Anna (known as Nannerl), was a fine pianist.

When Leopold realised just how gifted his children were, he decided to take them on a tour of Europe. It was an epic journey that lasted for four years, taking in Munich, Vienna, Paris, London, Amsterdam, Munich again, and finally Salzburg.

Mozart was just six when the tour began and by its end he was a star, having played in front of the most influential people wherever he had been. Throughout his life, Mozart was a keen letter-writer and many of his notes to friends and family survive today, giving us an authentic glimpse into his life.

As a child, Mozart learned fast how to wow an audience and could do all sorts of tricks at the piano. One of his favourites was to play with his hands hidden under a cloth, so that he was unable to see any of the notes. But he didn't just excel at performing; by the time he was 12 years old, he had already completed two operas.

It was time for Mozart to get back on the road again. On this occasion, the destination was Italy. The story goes that he heard a performance of Allegri's *Miserere* (see page 74). By papal decree, no printed parts existed for this work outside the confines of the Vatican. The young Mozart was so moved by the piece though that he rushed off and scribbled the whole work down on to manuscript paper, note perfect. This was a feat of pure musical genius. Although this particular tale is almost certainly apocryphal, it none the less bears repeating, as it's very much part of the Mozart legend.

While he was in Italy, Mozart was fascinated by the native opera composers and, by the end of his life, he himself had written some of the greatest examples of the genre, including *The Marriage of Figaro*, *Don Giovanni*, *Così Fan Tutte* and *The Magic Flute*.

Joseph Haydn was one of the great musical influences on Mozart's career, and each man was an unashamed fan of the other's work. Haydn told Mozart's father: 'I must tell you before God and as an honest man, that your son is the greatest composer I ever heard of.'

As a teenager, Mozart began working for the Prince Archbishop of Salzburg. It was always destined to be a troubled relationship, which culminated years later in Mozart literally being kicked out of the job with a boot up his backside.

Mozart spent his early years being lauded as a genius, and this took its toll on his relationships with those around him. He could be incredibly arrogant, and went through his life exhibiting a talent for upsetting people and for making enemies.

In love, Mozart was both pragmatic and persistent. When a young lady called Aloysia Weber spurned his advances, he turned his attention to her sister, Constanze, instead. A year later, they were married and they had children of their own. They stayed together for the rest of Mozart's life in a very strong and loving marriage.

Some composers need to spend hours working and reworking every note that they write, but Mozart was a very speedy composer, creating intensely tuneful melodies from scratch, seemingly plucking them out of the air at every turn. Once, when he was walking along the street, a beggar asked him for some money. Instead of tossing him a coin, he wrote out a tune on a piece of manuscript paper, telling the beggar to take it to a music publisher, who would exchange it for cash. Mozart himself said: 'I write as a sow piddles.'

Mozart was terrible when it came to looking after his finances. He worked hard and earned well for many years, but no matter how fast the money came in, he would always spend more than he had. During his final years, he was heavily in debt to many of his friends, who had no hope of ever seeing their loans again.

In the final year of his life, Mozart's health gradually deteriorated and there are all sorts of conspiracy theories about how Mozart came to die, including the idea that he was murdered by Antonio Salieri (as suggested in the play *Mozart and Salieri* and the film and play *Amadeus*). The story goes that a 'masked stranger' came to Mozart's door and commissioned him to write a requiem. The shadowy figure at the door was not in fact Salieri, but was instead a servant of a nobleman, who probably intended to pass off Mozart's work as his own. Mozart began to believe that the 'masked stranger' was the Devil himself and that the requiem was in fact for his own death. As he worked on the piece, his health worsened and he never managed to finish it. The final parts were completed by his pupil, Süssmayr.

Mozart left his finances in a parlous state when he died at the tragically young age of 35. He was buried in an unmarked grave just outside Vienna, leaving behind more than 650 different works, which showed his mastery of every type of classical music. Opera, symphonies, concertos, chamber works, choral pieces: whatever he turned his hand to, Mozart could write with aplomb. It was a sad end to a truly great composer's life.

+ AT A GLANCE +

LUDWIG VAN BEETHOVEN
BORN: 1770
DIED: 1827
NATIONALITY: German
MUST LISTEN: *SYMPHONY NO. 5*, WHICH MUST HAVE THE MOST FAMOUS OPENING BARS IN CLASSICAL MUSIC; *SYMPHONY NO. 6 ('PASTORAL')*; *SYMPHONY NO. 9 ('CHORAL')*; *PIANO SONATA NO. 14 ('MOONLIGHT')*; *FÜR ELISE*; *VIOLIN CONCERTO*; *PIANO CONCERTO NO. 5 ('EMPEROR')*; *FIDELIO*

It seems strange to have the two biggest names in classical music sitting side by side in this book. It has not happened by design and is purely an accident of their dates of birth. However, in many people's view, the pinnacle of classical music appears in these few pages covering the lives of Mozart and Beethoven. They might have a point, although there are plenty of gems still to come.

You might remember that, earlier on, we discussed the rather inexact science of deciding exactly where a period of classical music starts and where it ends. Well, Beethoven's music is a case in point, with his life straddling the end of the Classical period and the beginning of the Romantic period that followed. To illustrate this, it's worth looking at his symphonies as an example. His *Symphony No. 1* very much follows the form of those Classical symphonies written by Haydn and Mozart, but by the time his *Symphony No. 9* was premiered, Beethoven was writing music that sounded very different indeed.

Ludwig van Beethoven liked to claim that the 'van' in the middle of his name meant that he came from noble stock, but in fact he was descended from a perfectly normal family, with his ancestors originally coming from Holland.

There is no doubt that Beethoven had a tough childhood, though, and he was often beaten by his alcoholic father. He had obvious musical talent and his father was determined that he would become the 'new Mozart'.

Joseph Haydn taught Beethoven for a period, saying of him: 'This young man will in time fill the position of one of Europe's greatest composers, and I shall be proud to be able to speak of myself as his teacher.'

Unfortunately, Beethoven could be every bit as arrogant as Mozart – if not worse. He said Haydn was a teacher 'from whom I learned absolutely nothing'.

Beethoven was born 14 years after Mozart, and the young Ludwig played for Wolfgang, who was by then an adult. Mozart was impressed, saying: 'Keep your eye on him; one day he will make the world talk of him.'

In his twenties, Beethoven began to have trouble with his hearing, and by his forties he was completely deaf. He continued to create works of outstanding musicality and originality, without ever being able to hear a single note played. It is one of the most remarkable achievements in this whole book, and Beethoven should be marked as one of the very greatest classical composers for that reason alone. Yet Beethoven does not need to be shown any favours because of his disability. The music he created has stood the test of time and is regarded as among the greatest of the entire classical repertoire.

Although Beethoven refused to be defeated by his deafness, he did have trouble coming to terms with it. He would angrily thump the piano in an effort to hear the notes, sometimes even breaking the strings inside. He became an increasingly difficult person to be around, often drinking heavily, and he began to look increasingly unkempt, with wild hair and scruffy clothes.

Just as Mozart had done before him, Beethoven mastered a wide range of different types of classical music: from concertos to choral works, and from string quartets to pieces for solo instruments. He was a great concert pianist and wrote with an absolute understanding of what the instrument could achieve. Beethoven's best-known work for solo piano, the 'Moonlight' Sonata, wasn't given the name by Beethoven himself, acquiring it instead from a critic, who thought that the piece evoked an image of the moon over Lake Lucerne.

Unlike Mozart, Beethoven tended to take a long time to write each of his pieces. Mozart was able to dash off a new work incredibly quickly, whereas Beethoven liked to spend ages working on a new tune. He would often work things out in his head before finally writing it down. Then he would spend a long time crossing things out and trying new ideas before eventually settling on what he wanted.

Beethoven composed only one opera – *Fidelio* – and it took him years to get it right. He rewrote one aria no fewer than 18 times and came up with four different overtures before he settled on one that he liked.

Beethoven's speciality was the symphony – the style of which he developed hugely during his lifetime. For many, his final symphony – *No. 9* – was his biggest triumph, with a much larger orchestra, choir and four soloists. It includes the magnificent final movement, the 'Ode to Joy'.

By the time this piece was first performed in public, Beethoven was completely deaf. On the big night, he stood on stage with his back to the audience. At the end of the concert, it was only when one of the singers turned him around to face the crowd that he realised that they had been wildly cheering and applauding his masterpiece.

Beethoven was 56 years old when he died. His funeral was very different from that of Mozart. More than 30,000 people came out on to the streets to say goodbye. His torch-bearers included Franz Schubert – of whom more later.

Beethoven was a musical innovator. He led a troubled private life and never married, even though he fell hopelessly in love with a series of women. In addition to the problems caused by his deafness, Beethoven often had an unhappy time of it and he regularly became consumed with anger. Listening to music such as the *'Moonlight'* *Sonata,* this seems hard to believe. But, sadly it is true.

+ **AT A GLANCE** +

LOUIS SPOHR
BORN: 1784
DIED: 1859
NATIONALITY: GERMAN
MUST LISTEN: *CLARINET CONCERTO NO. 1*

Our final composer from the Classical period is almost completely eclipsed by the likes of Mozart and Beethoven, but nevertheless he was still an innovator in his own way. In fact, **Louis Spohr** was something of a revolutionary on the quiet. As well as being one of the first conductors to use a baton to keep time, he also invented the chin rest for the violin, some time around 1820.

Not only was he a well-respected composer, but Spohr was also a brilliant violinist in his day. He was widely admired as a teacher and his book, *Violin Tutor*, became required reading. Spohr was another of those composers whose output had one foot in the Classical period and the other in the Romantic period.

THE END OF THE CLASSICAL PERIOD

It might be the shortest period we cover in this book; however, this was a time that was by no means lacking in stature or importance in the overall development of classical music. The Classical years were marked out by some of the true greats. For the first time, composers became star names in their own right and, by the start of our next period, classical music had changed beyond all recognition from the style and forms that were the norms at the end of the Baroque period just 80 years before.

Gird your loins. It's time to get Romantic.

CHAPTER 7

THE ROMANTIC PERIOD

WHY ROMANTIC?

The Romantic period of classical music ran from around 1830 to 1910 or so. As with many labels used in this book, a strict definition of why Romantic music is romantic is quite hard to come by. There are parts of music written in all of the periods we cover that could be considered to be 'romantic'.

The composers whose work falls into this category tend to bring emotions to the fore in their music, and often use the notes they write to paint pictures in a very expressive way. This is different from those composers who came before them in the Classical period. For them, writing music tended to be about having a formal structure, or framework, within which to compose.

Having said all of this, there are composers from the Classical period who have elements of Romanticism in their music, just as there are composers from the Romantic period who have elements of Classicism in their music. Really, there is no hard and fast rule, just a series of general indicators.

WHAT ELSE WAS GOING ON IN THE WORLD?

History didn't stand still just because everyone was going all Romantic. Inventions during this period included socialism, postage stamps and the Salvation Army. Vitamins and radium were discovered;

the Suez Canal opened; Mr Daimler produced his first motorcar, and the Wright brothers flew in their flying machine. Radio was born when Marconi successfully sent a message by wireless to a receiver over a mile away; Queen Victoria celebrated her jubilee, and the Great Gold Rush got under way.

THE THREE AGES OF THE ROMANTICS

As you flick through this book, you might notice that this is the most substantial of all of the chapters so far, with no fewer than 37 composers included. Much of the music was composed in different countries simultaneously, and many of the composers' lives overlapped. To keep things as clear as possible, we have divided this chapter into three sections: The Early Romantics, The Nationalists and The Late Romantics.

THE EARLY ROMANTICS

These are the composers who bridged the gap between the Classical period and the later Romantic period. Many of them were alive at the same time as the Classical composers, and they were certainly influenced by the likes of Mozart and Beethoven. However, all of them moved on the development of classical music in their own way.

✦ AT A GLANCE ✦

NICCOLÒ PAGANINI
BORN: 1782
DIED: 1840
NATIONALITY: ITALIAN
MUST LISTEN: *VIOLIN CONCERTO NO. 1*;
VIOLIN CONCERTO NO. 2

Our first composer from the Romantic period was a superstar in his lifetime. During his performances, he was the consummate showman, able to perform all sorts of stunts using his violin. In the same way that Jimi Hendrix could amaze audiences more than a century later as a rock guitar virtuoso, **Niccolò Paganini** was able to stun those who saw him perform with his outrageously good playing.

Paganini could play complete works with just two strings on his violin instead of four. Sometimes, he would even deliberately snap some of the strings mid-performance – and still play the piece brilliantly.

Paganini's childhood was completely centred on music, and his father would punish him for not practising by withdrawing food and water. As an adult, Paganini's playing was so good that there were even stories suggesting that the only way anybody could possibly play the violin that well was if they had entered into a pact with the Devil. When he died, the Church initially refused to allow Paganini's body to be buried on its land for this reason.

Paganini was in no doubt about the benefits of being seen as a showman, saying: 'I'm not handsome, but when women hear me play, they come crawling to my feet.'

+ AT A GLANCE +

CARL MARIA VON WEBER
BORN: 1786
DIED: 1826
NATIONALITY: German
MUST LISTEN: CLARINET CONCERTO NO. 1

The style and structure of music was continuing to change in the operatic world, just as it was in music written for instrumentalists. In Germany, **Carl Maria von Weber** was at the vanguard of developments, although he lived outside the years that many people consider to be the Romantic period.

Opera was the family business as far as Weber was concerned, and he spent his childhood touring with the opera company that his father had set up. His opera *Der Freischütz* sealed his place in German musical history because of its use of folk tunes in the score. You will see a little later that this is an idea that became increasingly common in the Romantic period.

Weber also wrote a couple of cracking clarinet concertos – and it is for these that he is chiefly remembered today.

+ **AT A GLANCE** +

GIOACHINO ROSSINI
BORN: 1792
DIED: 1868
NATIONALITY: ITALIAN
MUST LISTEN: *THE BARBER OF SEVILLE*; *THE THIEVING MAGPIE*; *WILLIAM TELL*; *STABAT MATER*

Italy is the home of opera and in **Gioachino Rossini** the Italians had a new hero. He wrote both comic and tragic operas to equal acclaim.

Rossini was another of those composers who created new works very quickly, and it never seemed to take him longer than a few weeks to write an opera. At the height of his creative powers, he once said: 'Give me a laundry list and I will set it to music.'

Rossini claimed to have composed the whole of *The Barber of Seville* in just 13 days. His fast work rate meant that he had a stream of new operas premiering in opera houses across Italy. He did not always get on well with the interpreters of his creations, though, saying, 'How wonderful the opera world would be if there were no singers.'

Then, at the age of 37, Rossini suddenly stopped writing opera altogether, and in the final three decades of his life his only major work was the choral piece *Stabat Mater*. It's never been quite clear why he decided to do this, although by then his bank balance was particularly healthy following on from his enormous critical and financial successes around Europe.

Aside from the music, Rossini was a great lover of food and his name has been appended to more dishes than any other composer. Omelette Rossini and Salade Rossini sit alongside the ubiquitous Tournedos Rossini on menus. In case you're wondering, the last dish is made from steak layered on croutons with foie gras and truffles on top.

Now, our next composer liked to party the night away as much as the next chap, but he was by no means a slacker when it came to doing his day job.

+ AT A GLANCE +

FRANZ SCHUBERT
BORN: 1797
DIED: 1828
NATIONALITY: AUSTRIAN
MUST LISTEN: *AVE MARIA; MARCHE MILITAIRE NO. 1; OVERTURE
AND INCIDENTAL MUSIC TO ROSAMUNDE; PIANO QUINTET
('TROUT'); SYMPHONY NO. 5*

He may have lived for only 31 years, but **Franz Schubert** was a highly proficient composer by the time he was 17, and he still managed to leave behind more than 600 songs (known as 'Lieder'). Schubert also composed eight and a half symphonies, 11 operas and around 400 other pieces. In 1815 alone, he composed 144 songs, two masses, a symphony and a selection of other works.

All that composing didn't prevent Schubert from having a good time and he was famous for his musical parties, or 'Schubertiads', as they were known.

Schubert contracted syphilis in 1823 and died of typhus five years later in 1828. A year earlier, he had taken part in the funeral of his great hero Ludwig van Beethoven.

Interestingly, Schubert was one of the first major composers who relied on other people to promulgate their music. He himself only ever gave one major concert, in the year of his death, and this was overshadowed by Paganini, who had arrived in Vienna at the same time. So poor old Schubert was never really given the credit he deserved in his lifetime or in the years that followed his death.

One of the great mysteries of Schubert's life is his *Symphony No. 8*, which is known as the *'Unfinished' Symphony*. He completed the first two movements, and then abandoned it. Nobody is quite sure why, but it still remains one of his most popular works today.

+ AT A GLANCE +

HECTOR BERLIOZ
BORN: 1803
DIED: 1869
NATIONALITY: FRENCH
MUST LISTEN: *SYMPHONIE FANTASTIQUE*;
THE CHILDHOOD OF CHRIST; *REQUIEM*

Hector Berlioz's father was a doctor, and Berlioz didn't receive the sort of hot-housed musical education favoured by the parents of many of the other composers in *Everything You Ever Wanted To Know About Classical Music ... but were too afraid to ask.*

Berlioz actually began to train in Paris as a doctor himself, but ended up spending more and more time sneaking off to the opera. In the end, he switched courses to study music, much to his family's disgust.

Berlioz was almost a caricature of how non-composers think a composer should be: very highly strung with frequent temper tantrums; recklessly impulsive; capable of being intensely passionate, and, of course, absolutely hopelessly romantic when it came to falling in love. He once pursued an ex-lover with pistols and poison; he followed another disguised as a maid.

The principal object of Berlioz's desires was an actress called Harriet Smithson, whom he chased with a dedication that must have seriously unnerved her. He first saw her in a play in 1827, but didn't actually meet her until 1832. At first, she spurned his advances, and he wrote his *Symphonie Fantastique* as a response. They were finally married in 1833, but – true to form – he fell hopelessly in love with someone else within a few years.

When it came to writing music, Berlioz was not afraid to think big. Take his *Requiem*, for example. It was written for a huge orchestra and chorus, as well as four brass bands, one at each corner of the stage. This addiction to making everything as big as possible has not always stood Berlioz in good stead since his death. It means that it can be prohibitively expensive to stage his works in the way that he envisaged them because of the vast number of musicians who have to be paid. He knew his own mind, though, and composed with zeal, saying, 'Every composer knows the anguish and despair occasioned by forgetting ideas which one has no time to write down.'

+ AT A GLANCE +

FELIX MENDELSSOHN
BORN: 1809
DIED: 1847
NATIONALITY: GERMAN
MUST LISTEN: *O FOR THE WINGS OF A DOVE*; *SONGS WITHOUT WORDS*; *SYMPHONY NO. 4 ('ITALIAN')*; *VIOLIN CONCERTO*; *HEBRIDES OVERTURE*; *A MIDSUMMER NIGHT'S DREAM*

Anyone reading this book, who has not yet left school, would be forgiven for feeling a pang of jealousy when they come across the likes of **Felix Mendelssohn**. He was, as we have seen before in these pages, and will see again before the end of our story, a child prodigy.

Mendelssohn didn't just excel at music, though; he was one of those infuriating individuals who seem to be brilliant at just about anything they try: painting, poetry, sport, languages – he mastered them all.

Mendelssohn was lucky in that he was born into a wealthy family who were part of Berlin's 'arty set'. During his childhood, Mendelssohn met many of the city's most talented artists and musicians in his own home.

Mendelssohn made his public debut at the age of nine and by the time he was 16 he had composed his *Octet* for strings. A year later he wrote his overture to Shakespeare's *A Midsummer Night's Dream*. It would be another 17 years before Mendelssohn would complete the rest of his incidental music for the same play (including the *'Wedding March'*, which is a feature of many marriage services today).

Mendelssohn was a cultured man with a happy, stable marriage and five children. He worked hard and travelled widely, including to Scotland. He didn't seem to think too much of the place, saying. '[They] brew nothing but whisky, fog and foul weather.'

This did not stop him from writing two of his most loved works about the country. His *'Scottish' Symphony* was composed 13 years after his first trip there, and his *Hebrides Overture* is based in some parts on Scottish folk tunes.

Mendelssohn had other links to Britain, with his oratorio *Elijah* receiving its premiere in Birmingham in 1846. He even became friendly with Queen Victoria, and was Prince Albert's piano teacher for a short while.

Mendelssohn died at the tragically young age of 38. There was no question that he was pushing himself to the limit and was working too hard, but he never really got over the death of his beloved sister, Fanny, who was also a gifted musician.

✦ AT A GLANCE ✦

FRÉDÉRIC CHOPIN
BORN: 1810
DIED: 1849
NATIONALITY: POLISH
MUST LISTEN: *NOCTURNE IN E FLAT, OP. 9 NO. 2; PRELUDE NO. 15 ('RAINDROP'); WALTZ IN D FLAT, OP. 64 NO. 1 ('MINUTE'); PIANO CONCERTO NO. 1*

Here is another character who was a Romantic through and through. **Frédéric Chopin** did, however, show a dedication to one musical instrument, the like of which we see nowhere else in this book.

To say that Chopin loved the piano would be an understatement. He adored it, dedicating his life to taking piano composition and performance to new heights. In fact, he wrote virtually nothing else of note for any other instrument at all, other than when an orchestra was involved in a supporting role to a piano soloist.

Chopin was born in 1810 in Warsaw, to a French father and Polish mother. By the time he was just seven years old, he was already composing and performing; he never looked back.

Chopin became a fixture in Paris society, making good money by teaching rich people how to play the piano. He was fastidious about how he looked and always careful to ensure that he was wearing the most fashionable outfits.

As a composer, Chopin was particularly methodical. Not for him a hurried scribbling out of a new piece. Instead, composition was a rather painful and drawn-out process. He ended up writing 169 works for solo piano, and each one was finessed to perfection.

Chopin fell in love with a celebrated French writer with the remarkable name Amandine-Aurore-Lucile Dupin. She is better known under her male pseudonym, George Sand. She certainly sounds like a bit of a character. She could often be seen strutting about the streets of Paris wearing men's clothes and smoking a large cigar, much to the shock of polite society in the French capital. Chopin and Sand had a stormy relationship and eventually fell out of love.

Chopin was another of the Romantic composers who died young, claimed by tuberculosis at the age of 39, shortly after his relationship with Sand broke up.

✦ AT A GLANCE ✦

ROBERT SCHUMANN
BORN: 1810
DIED: 1856
NATIONALITY: GERMAN
**MUST LISTEN: *SCENES FROM CHILDHOOD (KINDERSZENEN)*;
'*DREAMING*'; *FANTASY IN C*; *PIANO CONCERTO*;
THE SONG-CYCLE *DICHTERLIEBE***

Robert Schumann was yet another composer whose life was a tale of tragedy and early death. He was a brilliant composer, but spent most of his life in the shadow of his wife **Clara Schumann**, who was one of the most famed pianists of the day. She was less well known as a composer, but wrote very attractive music.

Schumann was unable to follow his dream of becoming a concert pianist because of an injury to his hand, and he was not always happy to live in the shadow of his wife's celebrity.

He is best remembered today for his piano pieces, his songs and his chamber music. Schumann suffered from syphilis and depression, trying to commit suicide by throwing himself into the River Rhine. He was placed in an asylum, where he died two years later.

Schumann was pragmatic about his art, saying, 'In order to compose, all you have to do is remember a tune that nobody else thought of.'

+ AT A GLANCE +

FRANZ LISZT
BORN: 1811
DIED: 1886
NATIONALITY: HUNGARIAN
MUST LISTEN: *HUNGARIAN RHAPSODY NO. 2*; *LIEBESTRAUM NO. 3*; *PIANO CONCERTO NO. 2*; *RAPSODIE ESPAGNOLE*

If Paganini was the ultimate violin showman, then **Franz Liszt** steals the crown in the Romantic piano world. Liszt was also an influential teacher and was tireless in flagging up the work of other composers, particularly Wagner, whom we shall meet later in our story.

Liszt's piano compositions were fiendishly difficult to play – but he wrote them in the knowledge that he would be able to pull off even the seemingly impossible, because of his own brilliant musicianship.

As well as writing his own music, Liszt was adept at turning other people's big tunes into works for the piano. Pieces by Beethoven, Berlioz, Rossini and Schubert were all transcribed by Liszt; he then performed them with his customary style and panache.

Considering that these pieces were originally written for an orchestra, it is remarkable how Liszt manages to make them sound totally complete, even though he had reworked them for just one instrument.

Liszt was undoubtedly a superstar of his day and lived the rock 'n' roll lifestyle a good century or so before it was invented, with a string of sexual liaisons. His decision to take holy orders did nothing to dampen his ardour.

Lizst is also responsible for a change in concerts involving piano and orchestra, which is still in place today. He wanted his adoring fans to be able to see his hands flying up and down the keyboard, so he had the piano turned around. Before then, the pianists used to sit with their backs to the audience.

He might be most famous for his opera *Carmen*, but as you will see from our list on page 193, Classic FM listeners are in no doubt as to **Georges Bizet**'s best work. '*Au Fond du Temple Saint*' (known as '*The Pearl Fishers' Duet*') from his opera *The Pearl Fishers* has consistently been one of the most popular operatic works in the Classic FM Hall of Fame, since we began the chart back in 1996.

Bizet was another of those children who excelled in all things musical at a very young age. He had written his first symphony by the time he was just 17. He was also another composer who died tragically young, at the age of 36, probably of throat cancer.

Despite his great talent, poor Bizet never really saw the success that he deserved in his own lifetime. *The Pearl Fishers* had a rocky start, and *Carmen* caused something of a moral outrage among Paris' chattering classes. It really found favour with critics and audiences only in the years after Bizet's death. Since then, it has been performed in the most important opera houses the world over.

THE NATIONALISTS

Here is another one of those inexact definitions for you. All of our Romantic composers, and indeed many of our Baroque and Classical composers, could be argued to be 'nationalist' in one way or another.

However, we have grouped together the next 14 major composers (all from the Romantic period) because their music is written in a certain style that enables listeners who know a little about their classical music to identify the country of origin.

Sometimes these individual groups are referred to as 'nationalist schools of composers'. This is not a bad description – but think dolphins, rather than children sitting in a classroom. A school of dolphins appears to swim together in the same overall direction, although once you look very closely, you see that each of the animals takes a slightly different route, jumping up, diving down, or moving from left to right at different times from their fellow dolphins. It works exactly the same way with schools of composers; although they have common links, each is writing his own style of music.

The Russian School

+ **AT A GLANCE** +

MIKHAIL GLINKA
BORN: 1804
DIED: 1857
NATIONALITY: RUSSIAN
MUST LISTEN: *RUSSLAN AND LUDMILLA*; *KAMARINSKAYA*

If Russian music has a father figure, then **Mikhail Glinka** is the man. Nationalist composers incorporated the folk music of their native lands into their own music, and Glinka was influenced by the folk tunes that he was introduced to by his grandmother.

Unlike many of the prodigies who litter these pages, Glinka took up music in a serious way only in his late teens and early twenties. His first proper job was as a civil servant in the Ministry of Communications.

When he decided on a change of career, Glinka visited Italy, where he worked as a pianist. It was while he was there that he developed a deep love of opera. When he returned home, he penned his own first opera, *A Life for the Tsar*. Glinka was instantly heralded as the finest Russian composer of the time. His second opera, *Russlan and Ludmilla*, was nowhere near as successful immediately, although it has stood the test of time better.

Alexander Borodin was another composer who had a working life outside music. In fact, he was a much respected scientist. His first published work went under the splendid title: *On the Action of Ethyliodide on Hydrobenzamide and Amarien*. You will never hear it played on Classic FM, though, because it was a scientific paper and nothing to do with music at all.

+ AT A GLANCE +

ALEXANDER BORODIN
BORN: 1833
DIED: 1887
NATIONALITY: RUSSIAN
MUST LISTEN: *'POLOVTSIAN DANCES' FROM PRINCE IGOR*; *IN THE STEPPES OF CENTRAL ASIA*; *STRING QUARTET NO. 2*

Borodin was actually the illegitimate son of a Georgian prince. His mother cultivated Borodin's love of music and the arts in general, a passion that he managed to continue to develop throughout his life. He had around only 20 or so works published because he was so busy doing his day job, but these included symphonies, songs and chamber music.

Along with **César Cui**, **Mily Balakirev**, **Modest Mussorgsky** and **Nikolai Rimsky-Korsakov**, Borodin made up a group of Russians known as 'The Mighty Handful'. Their success was all the more remarkable because all of them actually had jobs away from the world of music – a big difference between them and virtually all of the other composers featured in this book.

Borodin is best known now for the *'Polovtsian Dances'* from his only opera, *Prince Igor*. It's worth pointing out that he never completed the opera himself (even though he spent 17 years working on it), and his friend Rimsky-Korsakov actually finished it off. More about him on pages 116–17.

+ AT A GLANCE +

MODEST MUSSORGSKY
BORN: 1839
DIED: 1881
NATIONALITY: RUSSIAN
MUST LISTEN: *NIGHT ON THE BARE MOUNTAIN*; *PICTURES AT AN EXHIBITION*; *BORIS GODUNOV*

For our money, Modest Mussorgsky was the most inventive and influential of 'The Mighty Handful', although he shared one or two of the demons that seem to be very common among truly creative people.

After leaving the army, Mussorgsky became a civil servant. In his younger days, he was quite a man about town, but he had a fiery temper and struggled with alcoholism throughout his adult life. For this reason, he is often pictured looking dishevelled with an unnaturally bright red nose.

Mussorgsky would often start writing pieces that were never finished. Sometimes, friends would try to help him out by completing them for him, although we can never be quite sure that these pieces actually turned out in the way he initially planned them. Rimsky-Korsakov orchestrated much of Mussorgsky's opera, *Boris Godunov*, and his big hit, *Night on the Bare Mountain* (which featured in the Disney film *Fantasia*). Mussorgsky's *Pictures at an Exhibition* was orchestrated by Maurice Ravel some years after Mussorgsky originally penned it for piano – and it is this version that is the most popular today.

Despite coming from a wealthy background and having huge talent both as a composer and as a pianist, Mussorgsky died in drink-induced poverty at the age of just 42.

✦ AT A GLANCE ✦

NIKOLAI RIMSKY-KORSAKOV
BORN: 1844
DIED: 1908
NATIONALITY: RUSSIAN
MUST LISTEN: *SCHEHERAZADE*; *FLIGHT OF THE BUMBLEBEE*; *CAPRICCIO ESPAGNOL*

Nikolai Rimsky-Korsakov's family expected him to go into the navy, and he did not disappoint. They were a little more surprised when he gave up his life on the ocean waves to become a composer and music professor a few years later. In fact, Rimsky-Korsakov had been writing music all along and even started composing his *Symphony No. 1* while at sea, stationed for part of the time off Gravesend in the Thames

Estuary. This has to be one of the least glamorous composing locations for any piece of music anywhere in this book.

As well as being remembered for his work sorting out Mussorgsky's music, Rimsky-Korsakov wrote 15 operas of his own, all of which centred around Russian themes, although he was also influenced by music from further afield. We can particularly hear this in his greatest work, *Scheherazade*, which is based on the story of *The Arabian Nights*. Rimsky-Korsakov had a real skill for writing music that showed off orchestras at their very best. In his work as a music professor, he wrote extensively on the subject, and influenced many of the Russian composers who followed him – most notably Stravinsky.

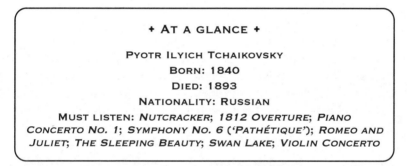

+ AT A GLANCE +

PYOTR ILYICH TCHAIKOVSKY
BORN: 1840
DIED: 1893
NATIONALITY: RUSSIAN
MUST LISTEN: *NUTCRACKER*; *1812 OVERTURE*; *PIANO CONCERTO NO. 1*; *SYMPHONY NO. 6* ('*PATHÉTIQUE*'); *ROMEO AND JULIET*; *THE SLEEPING BEAUTY*; *SWAN LAKE*; *VIOLIN CONCERTO*

Pyotr Ilyich Tchaikovsky took the Russian folk tunes favoured by the Russian nationalist composers, but he did something else with them, infusing them with other influences from across Europe.

Tchaikovsky led a tortured life, principally because of his homosexuality, and he died in mysterious circumstances. He himself said, 'Truly there would be reason to go mad if it were not for music.'

He was a delicate child and throughout adulthood was prone to depression, exhibiting suicidal tendencies on more than one occasion. After studying law, Tchaikovsky was employed briefly as a civil servant before leaving to further his musical studies. He made the mistake of getting married when he was 37 – a relationship that seems to have taken a terrible toll on both him and his wife. She ended up going mad and spending her last years in an asylum. For his part, Tchaikovsky became further depressed following the break-up of the relationship just two months after the wedding.

Tchaikovsky was particularly wounded by the poor reception given to his early compositions, and bad reviews also affected his mental state. It is ironic that many of the works involved, such as his *Violin Concerto* and his *Piano Concerto No. 1*, are great favourites today. Indeed, a recording of the *Piano Concerto No. 1* was one of the first classical records to achieve 'gold disc' status, selling millions of copies.

Tchaikovsky wrote ten operas, including *Eugene Onegin*, and ballet scores such as *Nutcracker*, *The Sleeping Beauty* and *Swan Lake*. Listening to these, nobody can be in any doubt that Tchaikovsky had a massive talent for creating highly melodic, catchy tunes – which is one of the main reasons that his ballets are performed so often today. These great tunes are equally in evidence when you listen to Tchaikovsky's symphonies and piano concertos.

For many years, Tchaikovsky benefited from the generosity of a rich widow called Nadezhda von Meck, who funded his work on the condition that the two of them should never meet. If ever their paths did cross, they agreed that they would not even acknowledge one another.

It is not entirely clear how Tchaikovsky died. Officially, he was poisoned by drinking water infected by cholera, although there is a school of thought that holds he deliberately took his own life because of fears over being embroiled in a homosexual scandal.

The Czech School

+ AT A GLANCE +

BEDŘICH SMETANA
BORN: 1824
DIED: 1884
NATIONALITY: CZECH
MUST LISTEN: 'VLTAVA' FROM MÁ VLAST; THE BARTERED BRIDE

If Glinka is the father of Russian music, then **Bedřich Smetana** occupies the same role for Czech music.

He constantly wove Czech stories and places into his music. There is no better example of this than his most popular work, *Má Vlast*, which translates as 'My Homeland'. It is a homage to the country of his birth, and took Smetana eight years to complete. Today, the most popular of the work's six sections is *'Vltava'*, which tells the story of the passage of the River Vltava through Prague.

Smetana ended up suffering from syphilis, deafness and, ultimately, insanity. He was, however, a huge influence on our next composer, **Antonín Dvořák**, although the latter's music won acclaim far beyond Czech borders.

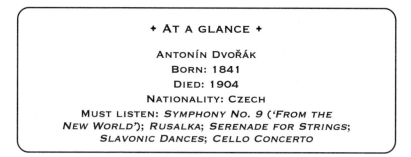

✦ AT A GLANCE ✦

ANTONÍN DVOŘÁK
BORN: 1841
DIED: 1904
NATIONALITY: CZECH
MUST LISTEN: *SYMPHONY NO. 9 ('FROM THE NEW WORLD')*; *RUSALKA*; *SERENADE FOR STRINGS*; *SLAVONIC DANCES*; *CELLO CONCERTO*

Dvořák was a Czech hero and he loved his homeland and its people with the same passion with which they adored him.

Dvořák's music was championed by the great Johannes Brahms, who is one of the big players later in this book (see page 130). Gradually Dvořák's fame spread around the world. He had a particularly solid fan base in England with commissions from the Royal Philharmonic Society and the Birmingham and Leeds Festivals.

Dvořák then decided to travel to the USA, where he was appointed Director of the National Conservatory of Music in New York in the 1890s. He was terribly homesick for the three years he was in the USA, but he did discover American folk music. He was influenced by these tunes when he was writing his *Symphony No. 9*, which carries the epithet *'From the New World'*. For an entire generation of British television viewers, the slow movement of this magnificent work will forever be known as 'the Hovis music', after its use in a highly memorable television advertising campaign for the bakery.

Dvořák felt the pull of his homeland throughout his time in the USA, and eventually he decided to go back home. He spent his final years working in Prague as a teacher.

Dvořák had one or two other interests outside music: he was an obsessive trainspotter and also developed a strong interest in ships. Indeed, this particular passion might have been one of the reasons he eventually agreed to travel to the USA in the first place, although the enormous riches on offer would have been another strong persuader. He was also something of a pigeon fancier.

Other composers in the Czech nationalist school include **Leoš Janáček**, **Josef Suk** and **Bohuslav Martinů**.

The Scandinavian School

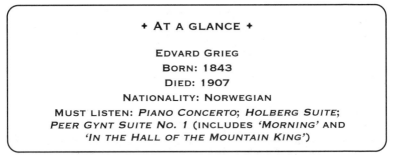

+ AT A GLANCE +

EDVARD GRIEG
BORN: 1843
DIED: 1907
NATIONALITY: NORWEGIAN
MUST LISTEN: *PIANO CONCERTO*; *HOLBERG SUITE*;
PEER GYNT SUITE NO. 1 (INCLUDES '*MORNING*' AND
'*IN THE HALL OF THE MOUNTAIN KING*')

The Norwegian **Edvard Grieg** was another of those composers who had a passionate love affair with the country of their birth. And his fellow Norwegians loved him just as much as he loved them. It could so easily have been very different, though. Grieg was actually of Scottish descent: his great-grandfather emigrated from Scotland to Scandinavia after the Battle of Culloden.

Grieg was best suited to writing small-scale works, such as his *Lyric Pieces* for solo piano, but his most famous concert work is his beautiful *Piano Concerto*, which includes a very dramatic opening with notes pouring from the piano over the top of a drum roll.

Other composers in the Scandinavian nationalist school include **Johan Svendsen** and **Carl Nielsen**.

The Spanish School

+ AT A GLANCE +

ISAAC ALBÉNIZ
BORN: 1860
DIED: 1909
NATIONALITY: SPANISH
MUST LISTEN: *SUITE ESPAÑOLA*; *IBERIA*

Although classical music was being written in Spain in the 19th century, the country was by no means a hotbed of famous composers. One exception is **Isaac Albéniz**, who was a bit of a tearaway as a youngster.

It's said that Albéniz could play the piano at just one year old. Three years later he was performing in public, and by the age of eight he was on the road plying his musical trade.

Albéniz was truly brilliant at improvising and could make up and vary tunes on the piano without a moment's thought. He often performed party pieces on the piano for money. He would stand with the keyboard behind him, and would play tunes with the backs of his hands. It is an incredibly difficult stunt to pull off. And, just for good measure, Albéniz used to do it dressed up as a musketeer, of all things. He had plenty of adventures as a youngster and by the time he was 15 he had already performed in countries as far afield as Argentina, Cuba, the USA and England.

As an adult, Albéniz led a far more conventional existence and became particularly famed for his very Spanish-sounding solo piano work, *Iberia*. His success brought Spanish music out of the shadows and to the attention of international audiences.

Albéniz was a big influence on many other composers from the Spanish nationalist school, including **Pablo Martín de Sarasate**, **Enrique Granados**, **Manuel de Falla** and **Heitor Villa-Lobos** (who was actually Brazilian).

The English School

+ AT A GLANCE +

ARTHUR SULLIVAN
BORN: 1842
DIED: 1900
NATIONALITY: BRITISH
MUST LISTEN: *HMS PINAFORE*; *THE MIKADO*;
IVANHOE; *SYMPHONY IN E*

It's been a while since we have been in England. In fact, **Arthur Sullivan** is the first English composer we have featured in the Romantic period. Come to that, there were no English names whatsoever in the list that we covered in the Classical period. We have to wind the clock back to George Frideric Handel for our last English composer of note; he died in 1759, and we borrowed him from the Germans, if we are being strictly accurate on the subject of origin. If you turn back through these pages, you will discover that it was Henry Purcell who was the last English-born composer to feature. And he began *de*-composing in 1695. We have had to wait an awfully long time before English composers have made it back onto the international stage.

The Germans were not slow in noticing England's failure to deliver the goods for a couple of hundred years. They took to referring to England as 'the land without music'.

Arthur Sullivan is still famous today. However, history has been rather unfair to him because he is best known for what might not actually have been his best work. In the 1870s, Sullivan began a partnership with the librettist W. S. Gilbert. They collaborated on a series of light-hearted operettas, including: *Trial by Jury*, *The Pirates of Penzance*, *HMS Pinafore*, *Princess Ida*, *The Mikado* and *The Yeoman of the Guard*.

Despite their enormous success, the two men never really saw eye to eye and had a series of extremely heated rows. One of their most spectacular bust-ups was about a new carpet at the Savoy Theatre in London, where their operettas were usually staged.

Sullivan was desperate to be treated as a serious composer, but by and large his non-operetta works are now forgotten. He wrote an opera, *Ivanhoe*, and an attractive *Symphony in E*. He also wrote the tune to the hymn *'Onward! Christian Soldiers'*, which probably now counts as his most performed work.

Other composers in the English nationalist school include **Hubert Parry**, **Charles Villiers Stanford**, **Samuel Coleridge-Taylor**, **Arnold Bax** and **George Butterworth**.

The French School

+ AT A GLANCE +

JACQUES OFFENBACH
BORN: 1819
DIED: 1880
NATIONALITY: FRENCH
MUST LISTEN: *THE TALES OF HOFFMANN*;
ORPHEUS IN THE UNDERWORLD

France's answer to Gilbert and Sullivan's English operettas came in the form of works by **Jacques Offenbach**, a man who obviously had a sense of humour. He was born in the town of Cologne and would sometimes sign himself as 'O. de Cologne'.

Offenbach also unleashed the can-can on an unsuspecting French public in 1858. The can-can comes from the operetta *Orpheus in the Underworld*, which scandalised the chattering classes of Paris at the time of its premiere. (You might have noticed by now that talkative types in the French capital seemed rather to enjoy being in a permanent state of shock and outrage at the artistic extravagances of one French composer or another.)

If you think the title of Offenbach's operetta sounds familiar, then you would be right. It is the same story that Peri, Monteverdi, Purcell and Gluck all set to music in previous centuries. Offenbach's version was very satirical, much more fun than the previous incarnations, and was riotously debauched in places. Despite the initial shock, it proved to be very successful and Offenbach never really looked back.

The other work for which he is most remembered is the more serious opera *The Tales of Hoffmann*, which features the 'Barcarolle'.

+ AT A GLANCE +

LÉO DELIBES
BORN: 1836
DIED: 1891
NATIONALITY: FRENCH
MUST LISTEN: *LAKMÉ*; *COPPÉLIA*; *SYLVIA*

By no means as influential as Offenbach, **Léo Delibes** is remembered now chiefly for his opera *Lakmé*, which includes 'The Flower Duet'. This was used to great effect in a long-running British Airways advertising campaign. Delibes also wrote two notable ballets, *Coppélia* and *Sylvia*.

Delibes was not without influential friends – he worked for both Berlioz and Bizet when he was chorus master at Paris's Théâtre Lyrique.

Other composers in the French nationalist school include: **Emmanuel Chabrier**; **Jules Massenet**, whose opera *Thaïs* includes the 'Meditation', which has become a party piece for many violin soloists; **Charles-Marie Widor**; and **Joseph Canteloube**.

The Viennese Waltz School

+ AT A GLANCE +

JOHANN STRAUSS SNR
BORN: 1804
DIED: 1849
NATIONALITY: AUSTRIAN
MUST LISTEN: *RADETZKY MARCH*

Our final two composers from among the Nationalist Romantics might well be father and son, but the time lag between the two generations was not great, with just 21 years separating the two men's birthdays. **Johann Strauss Snr** is known as 'the Father of the Waltz'. He was a fine violinist and set up an orchestra that toured all over Europe, with great financial success.

+ **AT A GLANCE** +

JOHANN STRAUSS JNR
BORN: 1825
DIED: 1899
NATIONALITY: AUSTRIAN
MUST LISTEN: *BY THE BEAUTIFUL BLUE DANUBE; DIE FLEDERMAUS; TALES FROM THE VIENNA WOODS; TRITSCH-TRATSCH POLKA; THUNDER AND LIGHTNING POLKA*

Johann Strauss Snr might have been 'the Father of the Waltz', but it was **Johann Strauss Jnr** who was to earn the title 'the Waltz King'. His father didn't want him to take up the violin, but the younger Strauss II did so anyway, going on to set up a new orchestra to rival that of his dad. Strauss Jnr had a keen business brain and soon he was earning serious riches.

In the process, Strauss Jnr wrote nearly 400 waltzes, including the most popular of them all, *By the Beautiful Blue Danube*. In the end, he had six Strauss orchestras running simultaneously, two of which were conducted by his brothers Josef and Eduard (each of whom had around 300 compositions to his name).

Strauss Jnr's waltzes and polkas were an instant hit in the coffee houses of Vienna, and their light, jaunty style proved to be popular all over Europe. Classical music enthusiasts who take themselves too seriously sometimes consider the Strauss family's oeuvre to be beneath them. Don't let them influence you! This family knew how to write a great tune that can lift your spirits and reverberate around your head for days after you first hear it. It's a concept that the wildly successful violinist and orchestral leader André Rieu has caught on to almost a century and a half after the Strausses were at their peak. As we mentioned earlier, he has become a multi-million-selling recording artist through his championing of the music of Johann Strauss Jnr and his contemporaries.

THE LATE ROMANTICS

Many of our final group of Romantic composers were still writing music well into the 20th century, but they appear in this chapter rather than the next because they still have that Romantic sound to their work.

It is worth noting that many of these Romantic composers had strong friendships with some of the other composers discussed in 'The Early Romantics' and 'The Nationalists' sections of this chapter.

It also bears saying once again that there was so much great music being composed at the same time in different countries around Europe that any attempt to group the composers together in this way will be, to a certain extent, completely subjective. Although most reference books are very clear on which composers belong in the Baroque and Classical eras, things start to become a little fuzzier around the edges when it comes to the end of the Romantic period and the beginning of the 20th century.

+ AT A GLANCE +

GIUSEPPE VERDI
BORN: 1813
DIED: 1901
NATIONALITY: ITALIAN
MUST LISTEN: 'CELESTE AIDA' AND 'THE GRAND MARCH'
FROM AIDA; OVERTURE TO LA FORZA DEL DESTINO;
'QUESTA O QUELLA' AND 'LA DONNA È MOBILE' FROM
RIGOLETTO; 'DRINKING SONG' FROM LA TRAVIATA;
'ANVIL CHORUS' FROM IL TROVATORE; 'CHORUS OF
THE HEBREW SLAVES' FROM NABUCCO;
'DIES IRAE' FROM THE REQUIEM

In 19th-century Italy, one opera composer stood head and shoulders above all others: **Giuseppe Verdi**. He had a big bushy moustache and beard, and photographs show him with a glint in his eye.

Verdi's operas are packed full of great tunes. In total, he wrote 26 operas, most of which are still being performed today. They include many of the best-known operatic arias of all time.

Verdi was a big hit with opera audiences across Italy, and when

Aida received its premiere, the standing ovation at the end was so prolonged that the company made no fewer than 32 curtain calls.

None the less, there was sadness in Verdi's life, too. He outlived both of his wives and two of his children. His music generated considerable wealth and when he died he left his riches to a retirement home for musicians, which he had had built in Milan. He said that he regarded this as a greater work than all of his music.

Although he is best known for his operas, no discussion of Verdi's life would be complete without mention of his *Requiem*. It is regarded as one of the greatest pieces of choral music of all time. Although it was always intended to be a purely choral work, it is full of drama and rather operatic in style.

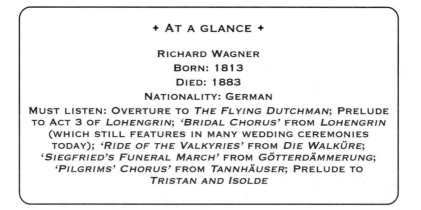

+ AT A GLANCE +

RICHARD WAGNER
BORN: 1813
DIED: 1883
NATIONALITY: GERMAN
MUST LISTEN: OVERTURE TO *THE FLYING DUTCHMAN*; PRELUDE TO ACT 3 OF *LOHENGRIN*; 'BRIDAL CHORUS' FROM *LOHENGRIN* (WHICH STILL FEATURES IN MANY WEDDING CEREMONIES TODAY); 'RIDE OF THE VALKYRIES' FROM *DIE WALKÜRE*; 'SIEGFRIED'S FUNERAL MARCH' FROM *GÖTTERDÄMMERUNG*; 'PILGRIMS' CHORUS' FROM *TANNHÄUSER*; PRELUDE TO *TRISTAN AND ISOLDE*

Our next composer was not a nice man. In fact, he was the most odious character with the most hateful views in the whole of this book. If we were choosing composers to include in this book in terms of their personalities, then **Richard Wagner** simply would not make it. However, we are judging the music – not the man – and so no history of classical music is complete without his inclusion.

Wagner's brilliance as a composer is not in doubt. Some of the most important and impressive music of the whole of the Romantic period came from his pen, especially in the world of opera. Yet he was an anti-Semitic racist, a serial philanderer, who was prepared to lie, cheat and steal to get what he wanted, and he would ride rough-shod over people, casting them aside without further thought. Wagner had a monstrous ego, a vile temper, was wildly eccentric and appeared almost to believe that he was some form of deity.

It is for his operas that Wagner is chiefly remembered. He took German opera to a whole new level and, although he was born in the same year as Verdi, the sound he created was very different from that of the Italian operas of the same period.

One of Wagner's big ideas was to give each of his main characters a musical theme that recurred in the music at the points when they were at the forefront of the action. (This is one of the first significant uses of a leitmotif that we discussed right back at the beginning of the book.) It might seem very logical to anyone who is a fan of musicals today, but at the time it was a revolutionary idea.

Wagner's greatest triumph was the *Ring* cycle, which is made up of four operas: *Das Rheingold*, *Die Walküre*, *Siegfried* and *Götterdämmerung*. These tend to be performed over four consecutive nights and last well in excess of 15 hours. These four operas represent a huge achievement for one man and, just because we find his views so objectionable, that should not take away from their magnificence.

Length is something of a trademark for Wagner. His final opera, *Parsifal*, is well over four hours long. The conductor, David Randolph, described it as 'the kind of opera that starts at six o'clock and after it has been going three hours you look at your watch and it says 6:20'.

✦ AT A GLANCE ✦

ANTON BRUCKNER
BORN: 1824
DIED: 1896
NATIONALITY: AUSTRIAN
MUST LISTEN: *SYMPHONY NO. 7*; *SYMPHONY NO. 8*; *LOCUS ISTE*

Anton Bruckner's life as a composer is a lesson in never giving up. He was a hard worker, thinking nothing of practising for 12 hours a day in his job as an organist. He taught himself much of what he knew about music and graduated from a correspondence course on composition at the ripe old age of 37.

Bruckner is most respected today for his symphonies – he wrote eleven of them in total. He was sometimes racked with self-doubt, but he did at least achieve acclamation, although much later in life than he deserved. The critics finally told him they loved him following the premiere of his *Symphony No. 7*. He was 60 years old.

✦ AT A GLANCE ✦

JOHANNES BRAHMS
BORN: 1833
DIED: 1897
NATIONALITY: GERMAN
MUST LISTEN: *ACADEMIC FESTIVAL OVERTURE*;
***HUNGARIAN DANCE NO. 5*; *PIANO CONCERTO NO. 1*;**
SYMPHONY NO. 4*; *VIOLIN CONCERTO

Johannes Brahms was not one of those composers born with a silver baton in his hands. Instead, he came from a relatively poor background, or at least from a good family who were no longer as rich as they had been. As a teenager, Brahms would earn money by playing the piano in brothels around his native Hamburg. It's fair to say that he had already seen something of the seedier side of life by the time he was an adult.

Brahms's music was championed by Robert Schumann, and the two men became friends. When Schumann died, Brahms grew closer to Clara Schumann, eventually falling passionately in love with her. It's not clear exactly how close they became, although Brahms's relationship with her might have coloured his judgement of other women, because nobody else seems to have held the same significance in his affections.

Brahms was quite a curt and short-tempered man, but his friends claimed that he had a softer side, which he did not always show towards strangers. On his way out of a party, he once said, 'If there is anyone here whom I have not insulted, I beg his pardon.'

Brahms would not have won any prizes in a 'best turned-out

composer' competition. He hated to buy new clothes and often wore baggy trousers that were covered in patches and nearly always too short. On one occasion, his trousers nearly fell down altogether in the middle of a performance. Another time, he was forced to take off his tie and use it as a belt to keep his trousers from ending up around his ankles.

Brahms's musical style owes much to the influences of Haydn, Mozart and Beethoven, and some music experts believe him to be a composer who still wrote in the style of the Classical period some years later than was strictly fashionable. That said, Brahms did introduce some new ideas. He was particularly adept at developing small groups of notes in his music and stretching them out throughout the piece – what musicians call a 'recurring motif'.

Brahms was not an opera man, but otherwise wrote excellent examples of just about every other genre of classical music. This has, quite rightly, meant that he is regarded as one of the giants among the composers in the whole of this chapter. His own view on his music was to the point: 'It is not hard to compose, but it is wonderfully hard to let the superfluous notes fall under the table.'

✦ AT A GLANCE ✦

MAX BRUCH
BORN: 1838
DIED: 1920
NATIONALITY: GERMAN
MUST LISTEN: *VIOLIN CONCERTO NO. 1; SCOTTISH FANTASY; KOL NIDREI; SYMPHONY NO. 3*

Born just five years after Brahms, **Max Bruch** would have been completely eclipsed by his fellow German had it not been for one piece of music – his *Violin Concerto No. 1*. Bruch himself recognised this fact when he said, with a modesty that is rare among composers, 'Fifty years from now, Brahms will loom up as one of the supremely great composers of all time, while I will be remembered for having written my G minor Violin Concerto.'

How right he was. But what a piece to be remembered for! Bruch did compose many other works – around 200 in all – especially a number of big choral pieces and some operas, which tend not to be performed that often today. His music is big on tunes, but he did nothing really to break new ground. In fact, he was not that keen on the music of his fellow composers who were trying to innovate.

In 1880, Bruch was appointed conductor of the Liverpool Philharmonic Orchestra, but three years later he was on a boat to new job in the USA. The orchestra's players were not great fans.

+ AT A GLANCE +

CAMILLE SAINT-SAËNS
BORN: 1835
DIED: 1921
NATIONALITY: FRENCH
MUST LISTEN: *CARNIVAL OF THE ANIMALS*; *DANSE MACABRE*; *VIOLIN SONATA NO. 1*; *SYMPHONY NO. 3 ('ORGAN')*

We have already come across a galaxy of prodigious stars, but Camille Saint-Saëns arguably tops the lot. When he was just two years old, Saint-Saëns could already play tunes on the piano – and he had mastered reading and writing, too. A year later, he started to pick out his own compositions on the piano. Just four years after that, he had added a mastery of lepidopterology to his talents (that's the study of butterflies and moths). By the time he was ten, Saint-Saëns had no problem at all in playing piano works by Mozart and Beethoven. His other areas of expertise included geology, astronomy and philosophy. There was no getting away from it – he was a clever kid.

After studying at the Paris Conservatoire, Saint-Saëns worked as an organist for many years. As he got older, he became more influential in French musical life, and ensured that the music of composers such as J. S. Bach, Mozart, Handel and Gluck all received regular performances.

Saint-Saëns's best-known work is *Carnival of the Animals*, which he banned from public performance during his lifetime. He was worried that he would not be taken seriously as a composer once the critics heard it. It's great fun, with the orchestra depicting a lion, hens and cocks, tortoises, an elephant, kangaroos, an aquarium, a jackass, a cuckoo, birds, pianists, fossils and a swan.

Some of Saint-Saëns's other music was written for less-often-heard combinations of instruments, including his famous *Symphony No. 3* (*'Organ'*), which was used in the film *Babe*.

✦ AT A GLANCE ✦

GABRIEL FAURÉ
BORN: 1845
DIED: 1924
NATIONALITY: FRENCH
MUST LISTEN: *REQUIEM*; *CANTIQUE DE JEAN RACINE*;
DOLLY SUITE; *INCIDENTAL MUSIC TO*
PELLÉAS ET MÉLISANDE

Saint-Saëns was an influence on other French composers, including **Gabriel Fauré**. The younger man took over from Saint-Saëns as organist of the Church of La Madeleine in Paris.

Although Fauré's talent was nowhere near as prodigious as his mentor's, he was also a fine pianist. He was not a wealthy man, and needed his job as organist, choirmaster and teacher to pay the bills. That meant relegating composition to his spare time but, despite this, he clocked up well over 250 published works. Some of these were a long time in their gestation: Fauré's *Requiem* took more than 20 years to write.

In 1905, Fauré was made director of the Paris Conservatoire and was accorded the status necessary for him to have a big say in the development of French music at the time. He retired 15 years later and struggled with his hearing late in life.

Today, Fauré is well respected outside France, although his music remains far more popular there than elsewhere.

For fans of English music, the arrival of **Edward Elgar** must have been something of a relief. Many musical historians regard him as the first significant English-born composer since Henry Purcell way back in the Baroque period, although we did stop off at Arthur Sullivan on our journey through classical music history, not to mention acquiring George Frideric Handel along the way.

+ AT A GLANCE +

EDWARD ELGAR
BORN: 1857
DIED: 1934
NATIONALITY: ENGLISH
MUST LISTEN: *ENIGMA VARIATIONS*; *CELLO CONCERTO*;
CHANSON DE MATIN*; *POMP AND CIRCUMSTANCE MARCH NO. 1
(*'LAND OF HOPE AND GLORY'*); *SALUT D'AMOUR*;
(*SERENADE*) *FOR STRINGS*

Elgar loved England dearly, particularly his native Worcestershire, where he spent most of his life, taking the beautiful countryside of the Malvern Hills as his inspiration.

His childhood was steeped in music: his father ran the local music shop in Worcester and was the organist at the local church. The young Elgar was taught the instrument by his father and by the time he was 12 years old, he was already the reserve organist at church services.

After a year working in a solicitor's office, Elgar decided to try to make his way in the far less financially secure world of music. He worked as a jobbing musician for a while, giving violin and piano lessons, playing the violin in local orchestras, and even doing a little conducting.

Gradually, Elgar's reputation as a composer grew, although it was a hard slog for him to break through into the public consciousness outside the area in which he lived. It was his *Variations on an Original Theme* that did the trick. This work is now better known as the *Enigma Variations*.

Elgar's music is now seen as being intensely English, and his work is often called into play at major national events. His *Cello Concerto* has a sense of the English countryside about it; 'Nimrod' from the *Enigma Variations* is often played at times of national remembrance; and his *Pomp and Circumstance March No. 1* is more commonly known as 'Land of Hope and Glory'.

Elgar was a private man who loved family life. He did, however, leave behind one other magnum opus – his big, bushy moustache. For many years it was a feature of the Bank of England's £20 notes. Apparently, the detail of his whiskers made the notes particularly hard for counterfeiters to copy.

+ AT A GLANCE +

GIACOMO PUCCINI
BORN: 1858
DIED: 1924
NATIONALITY: ITALIAN
MUST LISTEN: 'CHE GELIDA MANINA' AND 'O SOAVE FANCIULLA'
FROM LA BOHÈME; 'O MIO BABBINO CARO' FROM GIANNI
SCHICCHI; 'UN BEL DÌ' AND 'THE HUMMING
CHORUS' FROM MADAMA BUTTERFLY; 'NESSUN DORMA'
FROM TURANDOT; 'VISSI D'ARTE' FROM TOSCA

Back in Italy, **Giacomo Puccini** was the natural heir to Giuseppe Verdi at the top of the Italian opera composers' league.

Puccini's family had always been involved in church music, but after he saw a performance of Verdi's *Aida*, Puccini found the call of the opera too great to ignore.

After studying in Milan, Puccini's first big operatic success was *Manon Lescaut* in 1893. After that, he had success after success after success: *La Bohème* in 1896, *Tosca* in 1900 and *Madama Butterfly* in 1904.

In all, Puccini composed 12 operas, with *Turandot* his final one. He died with just a small part of the work still unwritten. This was completed by another composer but, at its premiere, the conductor Arturo Toscanini stopped the orchestra playing exactly at the point where Puccini stopped composing. He turned to the audience and said, 'Here, death triumphed over art.'

With Puccini's death and the premiere of *Turandot*, the Italian operatic composing tradition was also snuffed out. There are no more great Italian opera composers to come in our history of classical music. Who knows if the tradition will be rekindled again with a new, as yet undiscovered, talent in the future?

✦ AT A GLANCE ✦

GUSTAV MAHLER
BORN: 1860
DIED: 1911
NATIONALITY: AUSTRIAN
MUST LISTEN: *SYMPHONY NO. 1 ('TITAN'); SYMPHONY NO. 2 ('RESURRECTION'); SYMPHONY NO. 5* – PARTICULARLY THE *'ADAGIETTO'; SYMPHONY NO. 8* ('SYMPHONY OF A THOUSAND')

Gustav Mahler's fame during his lifetime was as a conductor rather than a composer. He tended to do the former during the winter and the latter during the summer.

The story goes that, as a boy, Mahler discovered a piano in his grandmother's attic. Just four years later, at the age of ten, he gave his first public performance.

Mahler studied at the Vienna Conservatoire, where he began composing. In 1897, he became conductor of the Vienna State Opera, a job he would hold with great success for the next ten years.

Mahler himself began to write three operas, although he never finished any of them. Today, we think of him as one of the great composers of symphonies. He is responsible for one of the big blockbusters of the genre, his *Symphony No. 8*, which has more than 1,000 musicians joining together in one way or another: as part of the orchestra, the enormous choir or as solo singers.

After his death, Mahler's music was out of fashion for nearly 50 years before it was revived in Britain and the USA in the second half of the 20th century.

Born in Germany, **Richard Strauss** was not part of the Viennese Strauss dynasty (pages 125–6). Although he lived for almost the whole of the first half of the 20th century, he is still regarded as one of the great German Romantics. His international standing fell when he decided to continue working in Germany after 1939, although he was acquitted of being a Nazi collaborator at the end of World War II.

Strauss was a fine conductor, which allowed him to develop an intimate understanding of just how orchestras worked. He put this insight into practice throughout his career as a composer. He was also keen to pass on his experience to other conductors, saying, 'Never look at the trombones, it only encourages them', and, 'Don't perspire while conducting, only the audience should get warm.'

+ AT A GLANCE +

RICHARD STRAUSS
BORN: 1864
DIED: 1949
NATIONALITY: GERMAN
MUST LISTEN: *ALSO SPRACH ZARATHUSTRA*;
FOUR LAST SONGS

Strauss is best remembered today for the opening to *Also Sprach Zarathustra*, which was used in the Stanley Kubrick film *2001: A Space Odyssey*, but he wrote some fine operas – among the best to come from Germany ever – including *Der Rosenkavalier*, *Salome* and *Ariadne auf Naxos*. He also composed the very beautiful *Four Last Songs* for voice and orchestra just a year before he died. They were not actually the last songs that Strauss wrote, but they serve as a fitting finale to his composing career.

+ AT A GLANCE +

JEAN SIBELIUS
BORN: 1865
DIED: 1957
NATIONALITY: FINNISH
MUST LISTEN: *KARELIA SUITE*; *THE SWAN OF TUONELA*;
FINLANDIA; *VALSE TRISTE*; *VIOLIN CONCERTO*;
SYMPHONY NO. 5

So far, the only major Scandinavian composer to feature in this journey through classical music has been the Norwegian Edvard Grieg. We return to Scandinavia now, and home in on Finland, where **Jean Sibelius** became a national musical hero.

Sibelius's music is infused with Finnish folk mythology. His greatest work, *Finlandia*, is seen by Finnish people as being musically representative of their homeland, in the same way that the English tend to see many of Elgar's works as embodying their national characteristics. Sibelius was, like Mahler, also regarded as a master of the symphony.

Away from music, Sibelius was a heavy drinker and smoker, and he suffered from throat cancer in his forties. He was also hopeless with money and was given a state pension so that he could continue composing without having to worry about his finances. More than 20 years before his death, Sibelius stopped composing any music at all. He lived out the rest of his days in a fairly solitary state. He had particularly strong views on those who were paid to comment on his work: 'Pay no attention to what the critics say. No statue has ever been put up to a critic.'

+ AT A GLANCE +

SERGEI RACHMANINOV
BORN: 1873
DIED: 1943
NATIONALITY: RUSSIAN
MUST LISTEN: *PIANO CONCERTO NO. 2; PIANO CONCERTO NO. 3; RHAPSODY ON A THEME OF PAGANINI; SYMPHONY NO. 2; VOCALISE*

Our final Late Romantic composer is another man who lived until the middle of the 20th century, and he actually composed many of his biggest hits in the 1900s. Yet he is still considered to be a Romantic composer – in fact, for our money, he was the most Romantic of the lot.

Sergei Rachmaninov was born into a family that was not as well off as it had once been. As a child, his musical talents were recognised and he was sent off to study, first in St Petersburg and then in Moscow.

Rachmaninov was a stunningly good pianist, and developed as a fine composer, writing his *Piano Concerto No. 1* when he was just 19. He also found time to pen his first opera, *Aleko*.

Rachmaninov was never the happiest soul, and many photographs show him looking decidedly grumpy in front of the camera.

It was something that his fellow Russian composer, Igor Stravinsky, noticed: 'Rachmaninov's immortalising totality was his scowl. He was a six-and-a-half-foot-tall scowl ... he was an awesome man.'

When Rachmaninov played for Tchaikovsky, the older man was so impressed that he gave him an 'A++++' on his score sheet – the highest marks ever given in the Moscow Conservatoire's history. Rachmaninov quickly became the talk of the town.

Nevertheless, things were not to go so well for Rachmaninov for too long. When his *Symphony No. 1* was premiered, it received a terrible panning from the critics and Rachmaninov sank into a deep depression. His work rate slowed considerably, and he started to have trouble composing anything at all.

In the end, Rachmaninov went to see a hypnotherapist called Dr Nikolai Dahl, who managed to set him back on the road to recovery. And, by 1901, Rachmaninov finished the piano concerto that he had been trying so hard to write for ages. He dedicated his work to Dr Dahl, and it was regarded as a triumph by Russian audiences. The new work was his *Piano Concerto No. 2*, which has been a favourite of classical music lovers across the world ever since. Indeed, when we combined together all of the votes from the past 16 years of our annual Classic FM Hall of Fame listeners' poll, we found that this piece of music was the winner at the top of the chart, by quite some margin. (See pages 193–201.)

Rachmaninov began to tour across Europe and to the USA. When he was in Russia, he continued working as a conductor and composer. Following the Russian Revolution in 1917, Rachmaninov took his family off on a tour of Scandinavia. He never went back home. Instead, he moved to Switzerland, where he had a house on the banks of Lake Lucerne. He had always loved rivers and boats and was, by now, a rich man.

Rachmaninov was a brilliant conductor and he had this advice for those who also wanted to excel in this field: 'A good conductor ought to be a good chauffeur. The qualities that make the one also make the other. They are concentration, an incessant control of attention, and presence of mind – the conductor only has to add a little sense of music.'

In 1935, Rachmaninov decided that he would make even more of a fortune by returning to the USA. First he lived in New York, before finally moving to Los Angeles. Once he was there, he set about building himself a new home that was absolutely identical to the one he had left behind in Moscow.

As he grew older, Rachmaninov conducted less and less – and composed hardly at all. It was as a pianist that he reached the height of his fame.

Despite missing his homeland, Rachmaninov enjoyed everything that the USA had to offer. He was incredibly proud of his large Cadillac, and often offered to drive guests home from his house, just so that he could show it off.

Just before he died, Rachmaninov became an American citizen. He was buried, not in Russia, but in his new homeland, in New York.

THE END OF THE ROMANTIC PERIOD

We have dedicated more pages to the Romantic period than to any other era of classical music. And for good reason – there was so much music being written in so many different places that the musical commentators of the time must have had trouble keeping up. There was a real change in the sound of classical music in this period, with the most popular composers ending up writing music with big, rich, lush orchestral sounds. In many ways, Rachmaninov best exemplifies this. When you think back to a composer such as Beethoven, who was still writing music at the start of the Romantic period, it's easy to see just how much things have changed.

However, if you think the sound of classical music changed during the 80 or so years of the Romantic period, then that is nothing to what happened afterwards. In the next period of classical music, things really started to sound very different – and not always for the better, either, in our opinion.

CHAPTER 8

THE 20th CENTURY

MODERN ... OR WHAT?

We are back to that issue of trying to label classical music again, and its stubborn resistance to being categorised into a series of boxes. The composers that we cover in this chapter were all writing music in the 20th century, and many books would consider them to be 'modern' or 'contemporary' composers. However, we're not quite sure that this sort of label is appropriate any more.

Consequently, we have divided the next two chapters into the 20th century and the 21st century, with those composers who have been writing music since the year 2000 in the second category.

For this reason, we are not convinced that we should refer to composers who have been dead for more than 70 or 80 years as being 'contemporary' or 'modern'. Maybe somebody will come up with a better title for these composers one day, but in the meantime we are gathering them under the heading 'The 20th Century'.

WHAT ELSE WAS GOING ON IN THE WORLD?

This was the century when the world became the place that we know now. Telephones, radios, television, widespread car ownership, international air travel, space exploration, home computers, compact discs, the internet – all of these developments changed the way in which people lived their lives.

Two world wars had a huge impact on society and international relations. This century also saw a change in the world order, with the USA and Russia taking on superpower status.

+ **AT A GLANCE** +

CLAUDE DEBUSSY
BORN: 1862
DIED: 1918
NATIONALITY: FRENCH
**MUST LISTEN: '*CLAIR DE LUNE*' FROM *SUITE BERGAMASQUE*;
LA MER; *PRÉLUDE À L'APRÈS-MIDI D'UN FAUNE***

Our first 20th-century composer, **Claude Debussy**, was an innovator through and through. He was responsible for changing all sorts of rules about how classical music should be written. Debussy lived in Paris, which was going through a phase of being at the very centre of classical music development during his lifetime.

While he was studying, Debussy showed a precocious talent for composing music with harmonies that were completely out of the ordinary. He is seen as an 'Impressionist' composer, and spent much of his time with the painters who were grouped together under the same heading.

Debussy took the inspiration for his music from paintings, works of literature and from the artists who lived around his flat in the Montmartre district of Paris. He was particularly fascinated with all things oriental.

Debussy had a complicated private life, with two of his lovers attempting to shoot themselves when he began relationships with new women. Ultimately, he fought a long battle with cancer. By the time he finally succumbed to the disease, Debussy had achieved widespread international fame.

Debussy's music was so different that when you listen to it and compare it with what had come before, it is easy to understand why he is seen as something of a torch-bearer for those composers who followed.

+ **AT A GLANCE** +

ERIK SATIE
BORN: 1866
DIED: 1925
NATIONALITY: FRENCH
MUST LISTEN: *GYMNOPÉDIES*; *GNOSSIENNES*

Another Frenchman, **Erik Satie**, took individualism in his music to the absolute extreme.

It would be fair to say that Satie was an odd man, and this was reflected in the titles that he gave to some of his works: *Veritable Flabby Preludes (for a Dog)*; *Sketches and Exasperations of a Big Boob Made of Wood*; *Five Grins or Mona Lisa's Moustache*; *Menus for Childish Purposes*; *Three Pear-Shaped Pieces* (there were seven of these); *Waltz of the Chocolate Almonds*; and *Things Seen from the Right and Left without Spectacles*.

One of Satie's strangest compositions is called *Vexations*. It is made up of the same few bars of music, which are played over and over again a total of 840 times. Unsurprisingly, this has never been a big concert hall hit, although every so often it is given an outing – usually more as a publicity stunt than a serious concert performance.

Satie's idiosyncrasies are also apparent in his ballet, *Parade*, which features parts for typewriter, whistle and siren. All this madness aside, he did write some beautiful solo piano works, including his famous *Gymnopédies*, although his sister Olga, who knew him as well as anyone, should probably have the last word on Erik: 'My brother was always difficult to understand. He doesn't seem to have been quite normal.'

+ AT A GLANCE +

MAURICE RAVEL
BORN: 1875
DIED: 1937
NATIONALITY: FRENCH
MUST LISTEN: *BOLÉRO; PAVANE POUR UNE INFANTE DÉFUNTE; DAPHNIS AND CHLOE; PIANO CONCERTO IN D FOR THE LEFT HAND; LE TOMBEAU DE COUPERIN*

We stay in France for our third composer of the 20th century. **Maurice Ravel** achieved unimaginable fame thanks to the decision by Jayne Torvill and Christopher Dean to choose his *Boléro* as their musical accompaniment as they skated their way to an Olympic gold medal and into the British sporting hall of fame in 1984. Almost three decades later, both the music and the skaters have been given a new lease of life on the prime-time ITV1 programme *Dancing on Ice*.

Another 'Impressionist' composer, Ravel was often clubbed together with Debussy. He was also a musical innovator and, again like Debussy, he did not always see eye to eye with the French musical Establishment.

A brilliant pianist, Ravel composed widely for the instrument, but for many people his ballet *Daphnis and Chloe* is his greatest work, despite the famous *Boléro* threatening to eclipse it in the public's mind.

Ravel was a short man and was not allowed to fight in the First World War. Instead, he worked as an ambulance driver and was deeply affected by the scenes of carnage that he witnessed. The sadness he felt is mirrored in the music he wrote at the time, such as the very moving *Le Tombeau de Couperin*.

+ AT A GLANCE +

RALPH VAUGHAN WILLIAMS
BORN: 1872
DIED: 1958
NATIONALITY: ENGLISH
MUST LISTEN: *FANTASIA ON A THEME BY THOMAS TALLIS; THE LARK ASCENDING; ENGLISH FOLKSONGS SUITE; FANTASIA ON GREENSLEEVES; SYMPHONY NO. 2 ('LONDON'); SYMPHONY NO. 5*

Leaving the eccentricities of France behind, we travel back across the Channel to England, to a man who must rank alongside Edward Elgar as the most English of composers.

Ralph Vaughan Williams was born in the very quaint sounding Gloucestershire village of Down Ampney. A pronunciation note before we get started: Vaughan Williams's first name rhymes with the word 'safe'.

Vaughan Williams began collecting traditional English folk songs from a young age. He used these tunes later in life as the central plank of man of his great successes. He studied at the Royal College of Music in London, at the same time as Gustav Holst. The two became lifelong friends.

Vaughan Williams wrote nine symphonies, six operas and a ballet, as well as numerous hymn tunes and scores for stage and screen. His music has deservedly seen a steady rise in popularity of the last 20 years, with *The Lark Ascending*, which is written for violin and orchestra, proving to be particularly popular among Classic FM listeners, regularly topping our annual Hall of Fame poll of listeners' classical music tastes. This piece is similar to many of his other works in the way in which it manages to paint a picture of the English countryside.

By the way, Ralph Vaughan Williams was not the only famous name in his family – his great uncle was Charles Darwin.

✦ AT A GLANCE ✦

GUSTAV HOLST
BORN: 1874
DIED: 1934
NATIONALITY: ENGLISH
MUST LISTEN: *THE PLANETS*; *ST PAUL'S SUITE*

Another Gloucestershire boy, **Gustav Holst** was born in Cheltenham, where his father was an organist and piano teacher. Holst was of Swedish descent, and his full name was Gustavus von Holst. He became concerned during World War I that he might be mistaken for being German, so he shortened his name.

A trombonist by trade, Holst turned out to be a very gifted teacher and, for many years, he was director of music at St Paul's School for Girls in London. He drew on English folk tunes for the inspiration for many of his works, although he was also inspired by subjects as far apart as astrology and the poetry of Thomas Hardy. Asked about his composing, Holst said, 'Never compose anything unless not composing it becomes a positive nuisance to you.'

It is easy to think of him as a 'one-hit wonder' today because of the enormous success of *The Planets*. Six of the seven movements represent the astrological influences of the planets: Mars (war), Venus (peace), Jupiter (jollity), Uranus (magic), Saturn (old age) and Neptune (mysticism). Mercury, the winged messenger of the gods, is the star of the other movement. You will notice that Pluto is not included in this list. The reason is simple – it had not yet been discovered at the time that Holst composed the work. (Composer Colin Matthews has plugged this gap and his *'Pluto'* is now sometimes played alongside Holst's suite.) Although *The Planets* is often performed as a complete work, *'Jupiter'* has a life all of its own as the tune to the great English rugby hymn *'I Vow to Thee My Country'*.

+ **AT A GLANCE** +

FREDERICK DELIUS
BORN: 1862
DIED: 1934
NATIONALITY: ENGLISH
MUST LISTEN: *LA CALINDA*; *ON HEARING THE FIRST CUCKOO IN SPRING*; *THE WALK TO THE PARADISE GARDEN*

The third of our trio of 20th-century English composers is Bradford's most famous son, **Frederick Delius**. His father was a prosperous wool merchant who didn't like the idea of his boy following a career in music. In an attempt to distract him from composing, Delius was sent to run an orange plantation in the USA. This actually had the opposite effect and inspired Delius to write *Appalachia*, which relies on African-American spirituals as its core.

While he was in the USA, Delius took lessons from an American organist, Thomas F. Ward. When he returned to Europe, Delius's father gave up fighting his son's musical aspirations and the young man was sent to study in Leipzig.

After that, Delius moved to Paris, where he spent much of the rest of his life. While he was there, he contracted syphilis, the symptoms of which made his life particularly unpleasant some 30 years later. He relied on a young Yorkshireman, Eric Fenby, to transcribe his final works.

Much of Delius's music is as English as it is possible for a piece of music to be. Take *Brigg Fair: An English Rhapsody*, for example. This set of variations is based on a folk song that hails from Lincolnshire.

✦ AT A GLANCE ✦

ARNOLD SCHOENBERG
BORN: 1874
DIED: 1951
NATIONALITY: AUSTRIAN
MUST LISTEN: *VERKLÄRTE NACHT*

Now, our next composer is somebody that it's impossible not to have a view about. Some people would say he should not appear in this book; others would say he is one of the greatest composers of the 20th century. Few people who have heard his music have no opinion at all. **Arnold Schoenberg** never really made it as a wildly popular composer among ordinary concert-goers, but he was very influential and widely admired by other composers.

At first, Schoenberg wrote pieces in the Romantic style, but then he developed a totally different way of composing, with a wholly new set of rules. Previously, composers had written music in various keys or sets of keys, with guidelines governing areas such as harmony and melody. These guidelines also had the effect of maintaining a gentleman's distance from dissonant or discordant music. Schoenberg threw these rules out of the window, in favour of a strict regime whereby no one note could be repeated until all other 11 notes had been played. (There are 12 notes in any one scale.) This equality between all 12 notes – called twelve-tone music, or serialism – often resulted in jarring or discordant music.

We play very little of Schoenberg's music on Classic FM because our listeners tell us that they don't like it. However, we have included him in this book because he was without doubt an incredibly important figure in 20th-century classical music, although the music he wrote is definitely an acquired taste.

It's important to stress that although other composers were influenced by Schoenberg, by no means all of them wrote music like him.

✦ AT A GLANCE ✦

BÉLA BARTÓK
BORN: 1881
DIED: 1945
NATIONALITY: HUNGARIAN
MUST LISTEN: *CONCERTO FOR ORCHESTRA*

There is only one other great Hungarian composer whom we cover in detail in this book – the marvellous piano virtuoso Franz Liszt. But **Béla Bartók** wrote music that was far more Hungarian-sounding than his predecessor did. In fact, Hungarian folk music became the abiding passion of Bartók's life.

Together with his great friend and fellow composer Zoltán Kodály, Bartók criss-crossed the country, gathering recordings of authentic Hungarian tunes on a primitive machine, which imprinted the sounds on wax cylinders. The two men kept careful records of everything they heard, producing one of the finest recorded archives of any country's music. Before this, tunes were passed from person to person and were not written down anywhere. As no recordings had previously been made, many of these tunes would have died out completely had it not been for the efforts of Bartók and Kodály.

Bartók became a music professor in Budapest, but he decided to leave the country with the onset of World War II. He took up a job at an American university, where he composed and gave piano concerts. Once there, he was not the hit he had been in his homeland and, in 1945, he died of leukaemia. Bartók left behind one particularly interesting work, his *Concerto for Orchestra*. Usually concertos are for a solo instrument and an orchestra, but Bartók believed that the Boston Symphony Orchestra, for whom it was written, was so great that it deserved to have a concerto composed for solo groupings from within the orchestra.

✦ AT A GLANCE ✦

IGOR STRAVINSKY
BORN: 1882
DIED: 1971
NATIONALITY: RUSSIAN
MUST LISTEN: *THE RITE OF SPRING; THE FIREBIRD*

Igor Stravinsky was a giant among 20th-century composers. He was always keen to innovate and was often at the forefront of new trends in the way that classical music was written.

Stravinsky was lucky enough to have Nikolai Rimsky-Korsakov as his teacher when he was a boy. He never received any other formal instruction in how to compose.

As an adult, Stravinsky's talents were spotted by the great ballet impresario, Sergei Diaghilev. He had the power to make or break composers. Diaghilev commissioned Stravinsky to write *The Firebird*, which was based on an old Russian folk story. It was a big hit.

Stravinsky's next commission for Diaghilev was *Petrushka* – another ballet and another massive critical and box office success. Things didn't go so well when the two men paired up once again though. Stravinsky's *Rite of Spring* caused mayhem at its premiere, with a riot breaking out in the audience. This was not just the odd murmuring of discontent, but full-on fighting. Half the audience was outraged by what it heard and the other half recognised Stravinsky's talent for innovation and was prepared to defend the work.

Stravinsky moved from Russia to Switzerland, and then to France, and finally to the USA, where he set up home, first in Hollywood and then in New York. He had never been afraid to reinvent himself musically, and his writing changed in style considerably over the years. At times he was particularly radical and during other periods he was more conformist to the classical music norms. These chameleon-like qualities extended to Stravinsky's life away from music as well. Along the way, he managed to change his nationality three times.

Stravinsky was always ready with a witty one-liner, whether talking about other composers, his audiences or just classical music in general. You will find him quoted in other places in this book, but here are two of his sayings that remain personal favourites: 'Too many pieces of music finish too long after the end', and, 'To listen is an effort, and just to hear is no merit. A duck hears also!'

+ **AT A GLANCE** +

SERGEI PROKOFIEV
BORN: 1891
DIED: 1953
NATIONALITY: RUSSIAN
MUST LISTEN: *ROMEO AND JULIET; LIEUTENANT KIJÉ; PETER AND THE WOLF; SYMPHONY NO.1 ('CLASSICAL'); THE LOVE FOR THREE ORANGES*

Another giant of 20th-century Russian music, **Sergei Prokofiev** was one of the many composing whizz-kids that we have featured in this book. In his case, he had managed to clock up two whole operas by the time he was 11.

After studying at St Petersburg Conservatoire, where he made a name for himself as a very challenging modernist composer, Prokofiev continued to write music that, to be frank, shocked his audiences. Like Stravinsky, he too was commissioned to write two ballet scores by Diaghilev, but neither enjoyed the great success of Stravinsky's big hits.

Prokofiev decided to move to the USA after Lenin took control in Russia, and he achieved major success as a concert pianist. He was commissioned to turn his piano work *The Love for Three Oranges* into an opera. It had a rocky beginning, but has eventually become one of his best-loved pieces – and certainly his most successful opera.

In 1936, Prokofiev decided to return home to Russia, but his timing was terrible as his arrival coincided with the period in which the state started to dictate what composers could and could not write. At one stage, Prokofiev faced charges of composing music that worked against the state, but he battled through.

It seems a rather cruel irony that Prokofiev died of a brain haemorrhage on the same day that Stalin – the man who had done so much to oppress his music over the years – also died.

✦ AT A GLANCE ✦

FRANCIS POULENC
BORN: 1899
DIED: 1963
NATIONALITY: FRENCH
MUST LISTEN: *GLORIA*; *THE STORY OF BABAR, THE LITTLE ELEPHANT*; *ORGAN CONCERTO*; *LES BICHES*

You might have seen this man's name on the side of pharmaceutical products because **Francis Poulenc**'s father was a wealthy chemist who owned the family firm Rhône-Poulenc.

Poulenc was the most famous of a group of French composers who were known as 'Les Six'. (The others were **Louis Durey**, **Darius Milhaud**, **Germaine Tailleferre**, **Arthur Honegger** and **Georges Auric**).

Poulenc became well known for his ballet *Les Biches*, and then for a long series of popular French songs. His composing style changed though, following the death of a friend. He became more religious and his music reflected his newly found faith. This period saw him write a number of religious works, including his magnificent *Gloria*.

Poulenc is also known to generations of children as the composer of *The Story of Babar, the Little Elephant*. It remains as good a way as any of introducing youngsters to classical music.

Our next trio of pre-war composers were all from the USA. Although we have mentioned America many times so far – particularly during the Romantic period – we have not yet featured any American composers.

Probably the biggest earner of all classical composers in his own lifetime, **George Gershwin** was banking as much as US$250,000 a year, which was no mean feat in the 1930s. He wrote a succession of very successful Broadway shows, film scores and orchestral works. A virtuoso pianist himself, he toured the USA and Europe.

With a background in writing hit musicals, Gershwin knew a good tune when he heard one, and his orchestral works, such as *Rhapsody in Blue* and *An American in Paris*, have show-stoppingly tuneful moments. His opera *Porgy and Bess* includes songs such as 'Summertime' and 'I Got Plenty o' Nuttin'', which are still performed with great regularity today.

They say that opposites attract and one of Gershwin's fans was none other than Arnold Schoenberg. It is hard to think of two men who wrote more contrasting music. In fact, the two played tennis together.

Our next composer holds the distinction of being the only one so far to have lived entirely in the 20th century. The son of New York Jewish immigrant parents, **Aaron Copland** was a musically talented teenager who decided he could learn more by studying in Paris. By the time he returned to New York, he had an idea that he wanted to develop a truly American sound to his music. Although it was without doubt classical music that he wrote, Copland managed to blend in elements of jazz and folk music.

Copland wrote a series of blockbuster ballet scores including *Billy the Kid*, *Rodeo* and *Appalachian Spring* – all of which are now regarded as being as American as apple pie. His *Fanfare for the Common Man* features at the inauguration of the President of the United States of America. Not bad for a guy whose parents were from Russia.

After World War II, Copland changed his writing style and started to adopt the 'serialism' advocated by Schoenberg. The pieces he wrote in this period of his life were nowhere near as popular as those that had come before, although he did once say, 'Composers tend to assume that everyone loves music. Surprisingly enough, everyone doesn't.'

+ AT A GLANCE +

SAMUEL BARBER
BORN: 1910
DIED: 1981
NATIONALITY: AMERICAN
MUST LISTEN: *ADAGIO FOR STRINGS*;
VIOLIN CONCERTO

Samuel Barber composed music that was Romantic in style, long after the Romantic period had disappeared. In fact, he was born in the year when we consider the Romantic period to have ended altogether.

Barber was not an innovator like Schoenberg, Stravinsky or Copland, and he certainly didn't write big showy tunes like Gershwin. Instead, he composed memorable melodies – but not too many of them, with only around 50 of his works published during his lifetime.

Barber is remembered today chiefly for his *Adagio for Strings*, which was used by Oliver Stone in his Vietnam War movie, *Platoon*; and for his *Violin Concerto*, which gives the soloist a particularly tough workout in its final movement.

✦ AT A GLANCE ✦

JOAQUÍN RODRIGO
BORN: 1901
DIED: 1999
NATIONALITY: SPANISH
MUST LISTEN: *CONCIERTO DE ARANJUEZ*;
FANTASIA PARA UN GENTILHOMBRE

Something of a 'one-hit wonder', **Joaquín Rodrigo** is famous for his *Concierto de Aranjuez*. He composed extensively for the guitar, although he was not actually a guitarist himself. His music did much to make it acceptable to treat the guitar as a serious classical instrument, appearing alongside the orchestra. Rodrigo was helped in this mission by two excellent exponents of his work: the British guitarist Julian Bream and the Australian guitarist John Williams. (Don't confuse this John Williams with the American composer of the same name; we meet the latter on pages 168–9.)

Rodrigo's music is filled with sunny Spanish tunes and, although he is remembered in the main for just one piece, his output was prodigious. He became blind at the age of three years, and composed all of his music using Braille. He always said that, had he not been blind, he would never have become a composer.

✦ AT A GLANCE ✦

WILLIAM WALTON
BORN: 1902
DIED: 1983
NATIONALITY: ENGLISH
**MUST LISTEN: *SPITFIRE PRELUDE AND FUGUE*; *CROWN
IMPERIAL*; *ORB AND SCEPTRE*; *BELSHAZZAR'S
FEAST*; *VIOLA CONCERTO*; *FAÇADE***

William Walton took over Edward Elgar's crown as the English composer that the Establishment loved the most. Born in Oldham, Walton spent a good deal of his childhood at Christ Church, Oxford, where he was a boy chorister. After studying music at Oxford University, he was lucky enough to find himself taken under the wing of the Sitwell family, an artistic and literary tribe, who took care of all his financial needs, allowing him to compose without having money worries.

When Walton was 19, he wrote *Façade* as an accompaniment to Edith Sitwell's rather outlandish and highly theatrical poetry. In his twenties, he wrote two of his other most important works – his *Viola Concerto* and *Belshazzar's Feast*, a breathtaking oratorio, which was premiered in Leeds.

Walton became a renowned film composer in the 1940s, and his Shakespearean collaborations with Laurence Olivier were particularly admired. He also wrote marches such as *Crown Imperial* and *Orb and Sceptre* for major state occasions.

✦ AT A GLANCE ✦

DMITRI SHOSTAKOVICH
BORN: 1906
DIED: 1975
NATIONALITY: RUSSIAN
MUST LISTEN: *JAZZ SUITES NOS. 1 AND 2*; '*ROMANCE*' FROM *THE GADFLY*; *THE ASSAULT ON BEAUTIFUL GORKY*; *SYMPHONY NO. 5*; *PIANO CONCERTO NO. 2*

Dmitri Shostakovich was another composer who, like William Walton, wrote a whole body of film soundtracks, including the very famous 'Romance' from *The Gadfly* and the less well-known *The Assault on Beautiful Gorky*.

Shostakovich was a graduate of the St Petersburg Conservatoire, where his *Symphony No. 1*, written while he was still a student, was hailed as a masterpiece. He fell foul of the state in 1934, though, when Stalin stormed out of a performance of his opera *Lady Macbeth of the Mtsensk District*. The review in the following day's *Pravda* was headed: 'Chaos instead of Music'. And the reviewer went on to brand Shostakovich as 'an enemy of the people'.

Shostakovich penned his *Symphony No. 5*, which is subtitled 'A Soviet Artist's Practical Creative Reply to Just Criticism', as a way of trying to get back into favour. It worked, and he was welcomed back into the fold, although he still had run-ins with the authorities later in his career, and he was creatively free once again only when Stalin died in 1953.

Shostakovich's music could be light and frothy, for example his *Jazz Suites*; or dark and dramatic, for example his *Symphony No. 7*. This epic work tells the story of the siege of Leningrad by the German army.

One interesting aside: Shostakovich also holds the distinction of having one of his songs sung by the cosmonaut Yuri Gagarin over the radio from his spacecraft to mission control down on planet earth.

✦ AT A GLANCE ✦

JOHN CAGE
BORN: 1912
DIED: 1992
NATIONALITY: AMERICAN
MUST LISTEN: IT'S TOUGH STUFF - GIVE HIS *SONATAS* AND *INTERLUDES* A LISTEN AND YOU'LL SEE WHAT WE MEAN.

Our next composer falls into the same category as Schoenberg. **John Cage** is not somebody whose music we often play on Classic FM. Again, this is because our listeners tell us that they are not overly fond of it. However, he was a big figure in 20th-century classical music, so he does deserve a mention in these pages.

Cage was one of the major experimentalists of classical music. He made it his life's work to explore different sounds that did not follow any of the rules that had developed over the years that this book covers. His music could be completely simple, or terribly complicated and chaotic.

Cage even created a new instrument – a 'prepared piano' – where pieces of metal and rubber are inserted into the body of the piano to create a completely different sound. He also used electronic tape in some of his pieces.

Cage's most notorious work is called 4'33" and is made up of four and a half minutes of absolute silence, where the pianist sits staring at the piano keyboard without playing a note. The 'music' is then supposed to be whatever other noises are heard in the background in the concert hall. Those in the know hail this as a magnificent concept. We think they may have missed out on having the story of the *Emperor's New Clothes* read to them when they were children.

✦ AT A GLANCE ✦

BENJAMIN BRITTEN
BORN: 1913
DIED: 1976
NATIONALITY: ENGLISH
MUST LISTEN: *THE YOUNG PERSON'S GUIDE TO THE ORCHESTRA*; *FOUR SEA INTERLUDES* FROM *PETER GRIMES*; *CEREMONY OF CAROLS*

Born in Lowestoft, **Benjamin Britten** had a consuming love of the county of Suffolk, spending the last 30 years of his life in the seaside village of Aldeburgh, where he began the Aldeburgh Festival. This is still one of England's annual musical highlights today. Britten lived with his lifelong partner, the tenor Peter Pears, for whom he wrote leading roles in many of his works.

Britten specialised in writing opera and vocal music, with the opera *Peter Grimes*, and his *War Requiem*, written for the consecration of the new Coventry Cathedral, being among his most highly regarded works. However, his most widely heard piece today could not be more different. *The Young Person's Guide to the Orchestra* was written as an introduction to each section of the orchestra for a documentary film made by the Crown Film Unit. Its original name was *Variations and Fugue on a Theme of Henry Purcell* – and the theme in question was taken from the incidental music that Purcell wrote for a play called *Abdelazar*.

Britten provided one of the best analogies we have seen to describe how composers go about their business: 'Composing is like driving down a foggy road toward a house. Slowly, you see more details of the house – the colour of the slates and bricks, the shape of the windows. The notes are the bricks and mortar of the house.'

Even though Britten was the first composer to be made a Life Peer, he could be surprisingly unstuffy about what life as a composer was really like: 'The old idea ... of a composer suddenly having a terrific idea and sitting up all night to write is nonsense. Night time is for sleeping.'

+ AT A GLANCE +

LEONARD BERNSTEIN
BORN: 1918
DIED: 1990
NATIONALITY: AMERICAN
MUST LISTEN: *CANDIDE*; *CHICHESTER PSALMS*;
WEST SIDE STORY

A larger-than-life character and a brilliant musician, **Leonard Bernstein**'s big tuneful hits could not have been more different from the music written by his fellow American, John Cage.

Bernstein was an accomplished pianist and a brilliant conductor, touring the world, working with the best orchestras, and spending 11 years as the principal conductor of the New York Philharmonic Orchestra. Bernstein was a master of composition and could as easily write a big populist Broadway hit such as *West Side Story* as he could create a beautifully poignant choral work such as *The Chichester Psalms*.

Bernstein was also the first composer to become a television and radio star, and he hosted regular 'Young People's Concerts' for much of his life.

When Bernstein conducted major concerts, his assistant would stand in the wings with a glass of whisky in one hand, a towel in the other, and a lit cigarette in his mouth. As soon as Bernstein finished his performance, he would rush off stage covered in sweat. He would grab the towel and wipe his face; down the

Scotch in one, and then take a huge drag on the cigarette, before charging back into the hall to rapturous applause from his adoring public.

CHAPTER 9

THE 21st CENTURY

TODAY'S BEST MUSIC

You could argue that the division between 20th-century and 21st-century composers is a purely arbitrary one. It would be true to say that many of the composers who follow enjoyed great success during the 20th century. However, we wanted to make a distinction in this book that you will not find in many other histories of classical music.

All the composers we feature in this chapter have composed a significant body of work in the 20th century. All of them have also made a contribution to 21st-century classical music, so we believe that, with the benefit of historical perspective, divisions between 20th-century and 21st-century composing may well be made. We're too close in terms of time to be sure where the musical historians of the future will place the dividing line between the end of one period of classical music and the beginning of the next, but we are sure that this line will be drawn, just as it has been in each of the periods we have covered in this book, right back to Early Music times.

+ AT A GLANCE +

PETER MAXWELL DAVIES
BORN: 1934
NATIONALITY: ENGLISH
MUST LISTEN: *FAREWELL TO STROMNESS*

When **Peter Maxwell Davies** was made Master of the Queen's Music in 2004, he followed a long line of illustrious composers in the job, including Edward Elgar.

Known to everyone simply as 'Max', Davies studied at the Royal Manchester College with a group of young British composers, such as Harrison Birtwistle, who were together labelled the 'Manchester School'.

Davies studied in Italy and the USA before returning to England as a school teacher. During his long career, he has written many works specifically for performance by school children. As well as an opera, *Taverner*, based on the life of the John Taverner we heard about back in Chapter 4 of this book, he has also written a stunning *Antarctic Symphony*, inspired by the time he spent literally at the bottom of the world.

Desolate landscapes must particularly appeal to Davies because he has lived on Orkney since 1971, with the islands and the sea providing huge musical inspiration over the years since. His most popular work among Classic FM listeners is *Farewell to Stromness*, a solo piano piece written as a protest against a nuclear reprocessing plant on one of the Orkney Isles.

+ AT A GLANCE +

HENRYK GÓRECKI
BORN: 1933
DIED: 2010
NATIONALITY: POLISH
MUST LISTEN: *SYMPHONY NO. 3*; *TOTUS TUUS*

The fame of **Henryk Górecki** rests on one particular work, his *Symphony No. 3*, which has the subtitle '*Symphony of Sorrowful*

Songs'. The recording made by the soprano Dawn Upshaw and the London Sinfonietta proved to be a massive hit back in 1992, when Classic FM began broadcasting. The words sung by the soprano, which Górecki set to music in the second movement of this symphony, were written on a cell wall of the Nazi Gestapo's headquarters by a young girl in World War II. The result is achingly beautiful and can be extraordinarily moving for the listener.

In the early part of his career, Górecki wrote many pieces that were quite experimental in their sound and very different from his later work. He had a strong religious belief, which particularly came to the fore in his music in the latter part of his life.

One quick note on his surname: it's not pronounced as it looks. The correct way of saying it is 'Goretski'.

+ AT A GLANCE +

ARVO PÄRT
BORN: 1935
NATIONALITY: ESTONIAN
MUST LISTEN: *SPIEGEL IM SPIEGEL*; *CANTUS IN MEMORIAM BENJAMIN BRITTEN*; *FRATRES*; *TABULA RASA*

If we were to start to try to identify 'schools' from within our 21st-century composers, then we would find that Henryk Górecki's music sits very comfortably alongside that of **Arvo Pärt** and **John Tavener**. All three men have made their names by composing ethereal-sounding choral music, which has its roots in their religious faith. Their album releases have been commercially successful, but this has come about more through listeners making a spiritual connection with the music than through any form of rampant consumerism on the part of the composers.

Pärt's earlier work was quite a tough listen, but in 1969 he stopped composing altogether for seven years after joining the Russian Orthodox Church. When he started writing again, his music took on the style that we know and love today. With its very clean, crisp sound, it has a sparseness about it, which makes it hauntingly beautiful – and extremely relaxing as well.

+ **AT A GLANCE** +

JOHN TAVENER
BORN: 1944
NATIONALITY: ENGLISH
MUST LISTEN: *THE PROTECTING VEIL; THE LAMB;*
SONG FOR ATHENE

Another religious man, John Tavener is a member of the Orthodox Christian faith. His music draws on the traditions of this religion, as well as Islamic and Indian music.

Remarkably, Tavener owes some of his early success to Ringo Starr. Tavener's brother was doing some building work for the legendary drummer and gave him a copy of Tavener's *Celtic Requiem*. Starr liked it so much that it was released on the Beatles' own Apple record label.

Tavener's music reached its widest audience many years later when his *Song for Athene* was used at the funeral service held at Westminster Abbey for Diana, Princess of Wales, in 1997.

Tavener often composes with a particular performer in mind, and he has written a number of works specifically for the soprano Patricia Rozario to sing. *The Protecting Veil*, one of his relatively few non-vocal works, was written for the cellist Steven Isserlis.

We have said it before, but it bears saying again. Don't confuse him with the John Taverner who was born in 1490. The clue as to who is who is in the spelling.

+ **AT A GLANCE** +

PHILIP GLASS
BORN: 1937
NATIONALITY: AMERICAN
MUST LISTEN: *VIOLIN CONCERTO; KOYAANISQATSI;*
THE HOURS; KUNDUN

During his long and distinguished career, **Philip Glass** has been successful at just about any type of classical music he has turned his hand to.

Glass studied at the Juilliard School in New York and also in Paris, before spending time learning about Indian music, a tradition that continues to fascinate him.

Glass is one of the driving forces behind minimalism, alongside Steve Reich and Terry Riley. This style of music is deceptively simple, often with a few notes repeated over and over again. The effect can be totally mesmerising for the listener.

Much of Glass's music has been first performed by his own group, the Philip Glass Ensemble, but he has also written for orchestras, with his *Violin Concerto* being by far his most widely heard concert work. His soundtrack for Stephen Daldry's film *The Hours* was another great success.

✦ AT A GLANCE ✦

JOHN RUTTER
BORN: 1945
NATIONALITY: ENGLISH
MUST LISTEN: *REQUIEM*; *A GAELIC BLESSING*; *FOR THE BEAUTY OF THE EARTH*; *CANDLELIGHT CAROL*; *SHEPHERD'S PIPE CAROL*

Enormously popular, **John Rutter**'s music is probably performed more often in more places than any other 21st-century composer. His bright and tuneful choral music has made him particularly famous across Britain and the USA. He has specialised in writing Christmas music to such an extent that it is now unusual to go to a carol concert and not hear at least one of his settings.

Like Peter Maxwell Davies, Rutter has often written music specifically to be performed by youngsters. His *Requiem*, which is arguably his greatest work, has become particularly popular with amateur singing groups, and the printed parts for this work are in constant demand by choirs and choral societies across Britain and the USA.

Based in Cambridge, Rutter founded the Cambridge Singers in

1979. They have since given many of the greatest performances of his work.

+ AT A GLANCE +

KARL JENKINS
BORN: 1944
NATIONALITY: WELSH
MUST LISTEN: *ADIEMUS: SONGS OF SANCTUARY*; *PALLADIO*;
'BENEDICTUS' AND *'SANCTUS'* FROM *THE ARMED MAN –
A MASS FOR PEACE*; *THE PEACEMAKERS*

Another highly commercially successful composer, the Welshman **Karl Jenkins** has written music that Classic FM listeners have taken straight to their hearts. He has regularly been the highest-ranked living British composer in our annual Classic FM Hall of Fame charts (see page 196 for more details).

After studying at the University of Wales and at the Royal Academy of Music, Jenkins began his career performing jazz and was a member of the 1970s band Soft Machine. He then moved into writing music for television adverts, winning many awards in the process.

It is as a classical composer that Jenkins is now famed. *Adiemus: Songs of Sanctuary* was the work that first propelled him to the top of the charts – a rare feat for any contemporary classical composer. Its catchy and instantly recognisable style made this fusion of choral and orchestral music a success around the world – it has notched up 17 platinum or gold album awards. Latterly, *Adiemus* has been eclipsed by another of Jenkins's works, *The Armed Man: A Mass for Peace*, which has a particularly beautiful cello solo in its *'Benedictus'*.

+ AT A GLANCE +

PAUL MCCARTNEY
BORN: 1942
NATIONALITY: ENGLISH
MUST LISTEN: *LIVERPOOL ORATORIO*; *STANDING STONE*;
WORKING CLASSICAL; *ECCE COR MEUM*; *OCEAN'S KINGDOM*

Think **Paul McCartney** and you don't necessarily think 'classical composer', but the former Beatle has carved out a successful classical music career alongside his rock and pop work. He has always had a knack for writing highly melodic music, and this is apparent throughout his classical pieces.

McCartney's first full-length foray into the world of classical music came with *Paul McCartney's Liverpool Oratorio*. This homage to McCartney's home city received its premiere in Liverpool Cathedral in 1991.

McCartney followed this up with *Working Classical*, an album of orchestral and chamber music, and *Standing Stone*, which revisited his earlier successes working with a choir and orchestra. At the end of 2006, McCartney released a new classical work, *Ecce Cor Meum*, an oratorio in four movements. Five years later, his first ballet, *Ocean's Kingdom*, received its premiere in New York.

An item of trivia for you: extracts from Beethoven's *Symphony No. 9* and Wagner's *Lohengrin* are both included in the Beatles' movie *Help*.

✦ AT A GLANCE ✦

LUDOVICO EINAUDI
BORN: 1955
NATIONALITY: ITALIAN
MUST LISTEN: *STANZE*; *LE ONDE*; *EDEN ROC*; *I GIORNI*

Ludovico Einaudi not only composes music, but he also gets on the road and performs it, with a particularly strong fan base in Britain, Germany and his native Italy. He trained in Milan, before being taught by the respected Italian composer **Luciano Berio**.

Einaudi's popularity is based largely on his solo piano albums; *Le Onde*, which was inspired by Virginia Woolf's novel *The Waves*; and by *I Giorni*, which followed on from his travels around Africa, particularly in Mali. He has also written soundtracks for a number of Italian films.

+ **AT A GLANCE** +

JOBY TALBOT
BORN: 1971
NATIONALITY: ENGLISH
MUST LISTEN: *THE DYING SWAN; THE HITCHIKER'S GUIDE
TO THE GALAXY; ONCE AROUND THE SUN*

Joby Talbot was Classic FM's first ever Composer in Residence. The album *Once Around the Sun* was the culmination of that year-long project.

A graduate of the Guildhall School of Music and Drama in London, Talbot was a member of the pop band The Divine Comedy before turning to composition of classical music, and film and television scores.

Talbot's film work includes scores for Alfred Hitchcock's *The Lodger* and for *The Hitchhiker's Guide to the Galaxy*, with his television work including the scores to *Robbie the Reindeer* and *The League of Gentlemen*.

+ **AT A GLANCE** +

PATRICK HAWES
BORN: 1958
NATIONALITY: ENGLISH
MUST LISTEN: *BLUE IN BLUE; INTO THE LIGHT;
HIGHGROVE SUITE*

Patrick Hawes took over from Joby Talbot as Classic FM's Composer in Residence in 2006, with his commissions for the radio station gathered together on the album *Into the Light*. In recent years, Hawes has emerged as one of the most popular contemporary English composers.

Hawes's debut album, *Blue in Blue*, made the fastest ever appearance of any work in the Classic FM Hall of Fame, entering the upper reaches of the chart just months after it was released. His beautiful choral piece '*Quanta Qualia*' has proved to be a particularly big hit, as has his *Highgrove Suite*, a work commissioned by HRH The Prince of Wales, which received its premiere in 2010.

Hawes's music follows the English Romantic tradition of Delius and Vaughan Williams, although Hawes has a particular interest in Renaissance and Baroque music – a subject that he studied at Durham University.

✦ AT A GLANCE ✦

HOWARD GOODALL
BORN: 1958
NATIONALITY: ENGLISH
MUST LISTEN: *'THE LORD IS MY SHEPHERD'* (THE THEME TO *THE VICAR OF DIBLEY*); *ETERNAL LIGHT: A REQUIEM*; *PELICAN IN THE WILDERNESS*

Howard Goodall's strong composing credentials were first established in musical theatre, although he has become among our most successful British film and television composers, with credits including *Blackadder*, *Mr Bean*, *Red Dwarf*, *The Catherine Tate Show*, *QI* and *The Vicar of Dibley*. However, it is for his choral music that he is best known to Classic FM listeners. He took over as the station's third Composer in Residence in 2008 and has also hosted a regularly weekly programme since then.

He wrote *Enchanted Voices*, an album based on the Beatitudes, which stormed to the top of the Specialist Classical Charts on its release and stayed there for months, winning a Classic FM Gramophone Award in the process. Goodall was named Composer of the Year at the Classical BRIT Awards in 2009, following the release of *Eternal Light: A Requiem*, which was incorporated into a ballet by the Ballet Rambert.

Howard has become a familiar face on television, regularly presenting programmes about music and the arts for Channel 4, ITV1, Sky Arts and the BBC, including his award-winning series *Howard Goodall's Big Bangs*. He has long been a passionate advocate of the benefits of music education and was England's first National Singing Ambassador.

+ AT A GLANCE +

PAUL MEALOR
BORN: 1975
NATIONALITY: WELSH
MUST LISTEN: *UBI CARITAS*; *A SPOTLESS ROSE*
(BOTH ON THE ALBUM *A TENDER LIGHT*)

The youngest composer in our book sprang into the nation's musical consciousness at the biggest event of 2011 – the wedding of the Duke and Duchess of Cambridge at Westminster Abbey. His motet *Ubi Caritas* was heard by 2.5 billion people around the world – the largest television audience in broadcasting history. At the end of 2011, he was a darling of the media once again after composing the music to '*Wherever You Are*', a choral work that stormed to the top of the charts after being recorded by the Military Wives. This choir, made up of wives and girlfriends of soldiers serving in Afghanistan, was put together by the inspirational choirmaster Gareth Malone.

Mealor studied music at the University of York and combines his work as a choral composer with life as an academic at the University of Aberdeen. The best collection of his music to date comes on the album *A Tender Light*, where it is performed by the choir Tenebrae under the direction of Nigel Short.

+ AT A GLANCE +

JOHN WILLIAMS
BORN: 1932
NATIONALITY: AMERICAN
MUST LISTEN: *STAR WARS*; *HARRY POTTER*; *SCHINDLER'S LIST*; *SUPERMAN*; *E.T.*; *RAIDERS OF THE LOST ARK*; *JAWS*; *WAR HORSE*

Our final group of 21st-century composers have all entered the public consciousness principally as writers of film soundtracks. As you may remember, back in the introduction to this book, we argued that these composers follow a long tradition of writing for film, which takes in the likes of Saint-Saëns, Copland, Vaughan Williams, Walton, Prokofiev and Shostakovich.

We begin with the undisputed celluloid king. So far, **John Williams** has written the music for more than 100 different movies. And there is no doubt that the rest of the film industry appreciates his talents: he has 45 Oscar nominations (the highest number for any living person), carrying off the statuette five times. He has been nominated for 22 Golden Globes, winning four times. Of his 59 Grammy Award nominations, he was victorious on 15 occasions. His mantelpiece must by now need some sort of structural reinforcement, such is the weight of his accolades.

Williams was born in New York in 1932, moving with his family to Los Angeles in 1948. He had loved music from when he was a boy and, after finishing his first set of studies, he joined the American Air Force.

Next, Williams moved back to New York for more studying, this time at the world famous Juilliard School. In the evenings, he made money working as a pianist in many of the jazz clubs in the city's Manhattan area.

Finally, Williams made the move back to Los Angeles, where he started to work in the film and television industry. Throughout the 1960s, he wrote the theme tunes of many successful American television programmes.

Then, in 1973, Williams met the film director Steven Spielberg, with whom he has subsequently enjoyed the greatest creative partnership of his long career. Their first film was called *Sugarland Express*. Since then, their list of credits includes blockbuster after blockbuster. Williams also collaborated very successfully with the *Star Wars* director, George Lucas, working on all six films in the series.

Despite the fact that he could choose to write his music using a computer programme, Williams prefers the old-fashioned way of composing. He uses a piano to work out the tune, and a pencil and paper to write down what he has composed. It's hard work, too – he might only have eight weeks to write around two hours of music for a full orchestra for a film.

+ AT A GLANCE +

JOHN BARRY
BORN: 1933
DIED: 2011
NATIONALITY: ENGLISH
MUST LISTEN: *OUT OF AFRICA*; *DANCES WITH WOLVES*; *THE BEYONDNESS OF THINGS*

Until his death in 2011, **John Barry** was Britain's answer to John Williams. Born in York, where his father owned a cinema business, Barry was always fascinated by the movies.

Barry's film soundtracks, spanning more than 30 years, include *Zulu*, *The Ipcress File*, *Born Free*, *Midnight Cowboy*, *King Kong*, *The Deep*, *Chaplin* and *Indecent Proposal*.

Barry is probably best known for his work on the James Bond films *From Russia with Love*, *Goldfinger*, *Thunderball*, *You Only Live Twice*, *On Her Majesty's Secret Service*, *Diamonds Are Forever*, *The Man with the Golden Gun*, *Octopussy*, *A View to a Kill* and *The Living Daylights*.

Barry's greatest classical scores are *Out of Africa* from 1985 and *Dances with Wolves* from 1990. It is no accident that both these films feature wide open landscape photography – just the sort of images that blend perfectly with Barry's lush, epic scores. The director of *Out of Africa*, Sydney Pollack, said of John Barry, 'You can't listen to his music without seeing movies in your head.'

The film earned Barry his fourth Oscar, a Grammy Award for Best Instrumental Composition and a Golden Globe Award. *Dances with Wolves* won him his fifth Oscar and another Grammy Award for Best Instrumental Composition.

The Beyondness of Things was Barry's first album of classical music not written as a film soundtrack. The absence of pictures did nothing to dampen his ability to compose great tunes.

+ AT A GLANCE +

HOWARD SHORE
BORN: 1946
NATIONALITY: CANADIAN
MUST LISTEN: *THE LORD OF THE RINGS*; *GANGS OF NEW YORK*; *THE AVIATOR*; *PANIC ROOM*; *THE SILENCE OF THE LAMBS*

No list of 21st-century film composers would be complete without mention of the Canadian **Howard Shore**. He wrote the soundtracks to all three movies that make up Peter Jackson's *Lord of the Rings* trilogy. When we ask Classic FM listeners to vote for their all-time favourite film soundtracks, it is *Lord of the Rings* that consistently tops the poll.

More recently, Shore has busy working on more music for J. R. R. Tolkien's fantasy stories. The producers of *The Hobbit: An Unexpected Journey* and *The Hobbit: There and Back Again* have stuck with the winning musical formula, by commissioning Shore to provide the soundtracks.

A little trivia for you: Shore himself is rumoured to make a cameo appearance as a Rohan Guard in the extended DVD edition of *The Lord of the Rings: The Return of the King*.

+ AT A GLANCE +

JAMES HORNER
BORN: 1953
NATIONALITY: AMERICAN
MUST LISTEN: *TITANIC*; *APOLLO 13*; *BRAVEHEART*; *FIELD OF DREAMS*; *A BEAUTIFUL MIND*; *THE PERFECT STORM*; *THE MISSING*; *THE MASK OF ZORRO*; *IRIS*

Born in America, **James Horner** started playing the piano when he was five years old and trained at the Royal College of Music in London before moving back to California, where he studied for a series of music degrees, culminating in a doctorate in Music Composition and Theory.

Horner's first major film soundtrack was *Star Trek: The Wrath of Khan* in 1982, and since then he has worked with film directors such as Steven Spielberg, Oliver Stone and Ron Howard, scoring more than 100 films.

One of the most commercially successful film composers, Horner has won two Oscars, two Golden Globes and three Grammy Awards. He has a further eight Oscar nominations, seven Golden Globe nominations and four Grammy Award nominations to his name. His best-known work by a long, long way is *Titanic*.

✦ AT A GLANCE ✦

HANS ZIMMER
BORN: 1957
NATIONALITY: GERMAN
MUST LISTEN: *GLADIATOR; PIRATES OF THE CARIBBEAN; MISSION IMPOSSIBLE; THE LAST SAMURAI; RAIN MAN; PEARL HARBOR; DRIVING MISS DAISY; THE LION KING; MY BEAUTIFUL LAUNDERETTE*

A brilliant musician as a child in Frankfurt, **Hans Zimmer** began his career in the world of pop music, working in the band Buggles. Their hit '*Video Killed the Radio Star*' was the first ever video to be broadcast on MTV.

Zimmer worked as an assistant to the composer **Stanley Myers** and had early success as the writer of television theme tunes. As a film composer, he has made his name for his skilful combination of electronic music with a traditional orchestral sound. His biggest success has been the soundtrack to *Gladiator*, which has sold more than 3 million copies around the globe. He also provided the scores for the second, third and fourth films in the hugely successful *Pirates of the Caribbean* franchise.

THE FUTURE

And so there we end our journey through the history of classical music – a journey that has lasted for more than 1,600 years so far, and we are confident that there is plenty more to come.

We started way back with Ambrose and Gregory sorting out the rules of plainsong, and then we travelled through musical time, taking in the Medieval, Renaissance, Baroque, Classical and Romantic periods along the way, ending up with the music of the past 100 years.

Is classical music struggling to find its place in the 21st-century world? On the contrary, classical music and the people who compose and perform it are in the rudest of health. It's worth noting that, of the 107 composers who we've featured in detail in our classical music chronology, 45 of them were alive at some point in the past 100 years. That sounds to us like an art form that is continuing to reinvent itself and to thrive.

The music of the great composers, such as J. S. Bach, Mozart and Beethoven, is as relevant to our lives right now as it was on the day that it was written. One of the most exciting parts of life in the classical music industry is the thrill of discovering a work of brilliance, which you can then share with other people. All the time new composers are coming along, writing new pieces that will become central parts of books just like this in the future. At the same time, new young performers are coming to the fore, providing modern interpretations of the music of the great composers, and championing fresh young talent.

Classical music is very much alive and well. It will go on changing its shape and sound for as long as there are people with ears to listen.

This final part of our book is more of a reference section. We don't really expect you to read it through from start to finish. Instead, we hope that you'll find it useful to dip into now and again.

We've included a full rundown of the Classic FM Hall of Fame, a list of classical music that you'll find in films and some suggestions about where you can look to find out more about the wonderful world of classical music. We've even included a selection of our favourite quotations uttered by composers about one another.

But, to allow you to put everything into historical context, Part III begins with a timeline that lets you see everything in order in one place.

CHAPTER 10

WHO WAS COMPOSING WHAT WHEN?

This timeline brings together in one continuous chart all the composers featured in this book, allowing you to see whose life crossed over with whose. Classical music doesn't exist in isolation, so the fourth column features a list of events that took place around the world in the year of each composer's birth or death.

Don't be confused by where a composer sits in relation to the beginning of each of the eras. In most cases, our composers didn't become well known for their music until adulthood, so you will find that in some instances their lives straddle more than one era. If in doubt, do refer back to Chapters 4 to 9.

Year	Who was born?	Who died?	What else was going on in the world?
♩ ♫ ♪	THE EARLY MUSIC PERIOD		♩ ♫ ♪
1098	HILDEGARD OF BINGEN		ST ROBERT FOUNDS THE FIRST CISTERCIAN MONASTERY AT CÎTEAUX, FRANCE

1179		HILDEGARD OF BINGEN	GRAND ASSIZE OF WINDSOR, INCREASING THE POWER OF THE ENGLISH ROYAL COURTS
1300	GUILLAUME DE MACHAUT		WENCESLAS II IS CROWNED KING OF POLAND
1377		GUILLAUME DE MACHAUT	POPE GREGORY XI RETURNS TO ROME, ENDING THE BABYLONIAN CAPTIVITY IN AVIGNON
1390	JOHN DUNSTABLE		ROBERT III IS CROWNED KING OF SCOTLAND
1397	GUILLAUME DUFAY		DENMARK, NORWAY AND SWEDEN ARE UNITED UNDER ONE CROWN
1453		JOHN DUNSTABLE	THE END OF THE HUNDRED YEARS WAR
1474		GUILLAUME DUFAY	GERMAN ASTRONOMER REGIOMONTANUS DESCRIBES HOW TO FIND LONGITUDE BY USING LUNAR DISTANCES
1490	JOHN TAVERNER		PRINTING OF BOOKS ON PAPER BECOMES MORE COMMON IN EUROPE
1505	THOMAS TALLIS		THE PORTUGUESE FOUND MOZAMBIQUE
1525	GIOVANNI PIERLUIGI DA PALESTRINA		BATTLE OF PAVIA – THE IMPERIALISTS CAPTURE FRANCIS I

1540	WILLIAM BYRD		HENRY VIII MARRIES AND DIVORCES ANNE OF CLEVES, AND THEN MARRIES CATHERINE HOWARD
1545		JOHN TAVERNER	POPE JOHN III SETS OUT TO REFORM THE CATHOLIC CHURCH THROUGH THE COUNCIL OF TRENT
1561	JACOPO PERI		MARY QUEEN OF SCOTS RETURNS TO SCOTLAND
1567	CLAUDIO MONTEVERDI		JAMES VI BECOMES KING OF SCOTLAND
1582	GREGORIO ALLEGRI		POPE GREGORY XIII INTRODUCES THE GREGORIAN CALENDAR
1583	ORLANDO GIBBONS		FIRST LIFE INSURANCE POLICY IS TAKEN OUT
1585		THOMAS TALLIS	ENGLISH TROOPS INVOLVED IN THE SPANISH-DUTCH WAR
1594		GIOVANNI PIERLUIGI DA PALESTRINA	HENRI IV IS CROWNED KING OF FRANCE
♩ ♫ ♪	THE BAROQUE PERIOD	♩ ♫ ♪	
1623		WILLIAM BYRD	THE DUTCH MASSACRE THE ENGLISH AT AMBOINA IN THE MOLUCCAS ISLANDS
1625		ORLANDO GIBBONS	CHARLES I BECOMES KING OF ENGLAND

1632	Jean-Baptiste Lully		The Swedes win the Battle of Lützen, but Gustavus Adolphus II is killed
1633		Jacopo Peri	William Laud becomes Archbishop of Canterbury
1643	Marc-Antoine Charpentier	Claudio Monteverdi	Louis XIV is crowned King of France at the age of just five
1652		Gregorio Allegri	The first Anglo-Dutch war begins
1653	Arcangelo Corelli Johann Pachelbel		Oliver Cromwell becomes the Lord Protector of England
1659	Henry Purcell		France replaces Spain as the European superpower
1671	Tomaso Giovanni Albinoni		Uprisings by peasants and Cossacks in Russia come to an end
1678	Antonio Vivaldi		Titus Oates wrongly claims that Catholics have been plotting to murder Charles II
1681	Georg Philipp Telemann		Charles II begins rule without parliament
1685	Domenico Scarlatti George Frideric Handel Johann Sebastian Bach		James II crowned King of England – in Scotland he is James VII

WHO WAS COMPOSING WHAT WHEN?

1687		JEAN-BAPTISTE LULLY	JAMES II OF ENGLAND EXTENDS TOLERATION TO ALL RELIGIONS
1688	DOMENICO ZIPOLI		ENGLAND'S 'GLORIOUS REVOLUTION'
1695		HENRY PURCELL	THE FREEDOM OF THE PRESS IS ESTABLISHED IN ENGLAND
1704		MARC-ANTOINE CHARPENTIER	DUKE OF CHARPENTIER MARLBOROUGH DEFEATS FRANCE AT THE BATTLE OF BLENHEIM
1706		JOHANN PACHELBEL	DUKE OF MARLBOROUGH DEFEATS FRANCE AT THE BATTLE OF RAMILLIES
1713		ARCANGELO CORELLI	TREATY OF UTRECHT ENDS WAR OF SPANISH SUCCESSION
1714	CHRISTOPH WILLIBALD VON GLUCK CARL PHILIPP EMANUEL BACH		GEORGE I IS CROWNED KING OF GREAT BRITAIN AND IRELAND
1726		DOMENICO ZIPOLI	CARDINAL FLEURY BECOMES CHIEF MINISTER IN FRANCE
1732	JOSEPH HAYDN		GEORGE WASHINGTON IS BORN
1735	JOHANN CHRISTIAN BACH		WAR OF POLISH SUCCESSION ENDS
1739	KARL DITTERS VON DITTERSDORF		WAR OF JENKINS' EAR BETWEEN BRITAIN AND SPAIN

1741		ANTONIO VIVALDI	SWEDEN AND RUSSIA AT WAR
1743	LUIGI BOCCHERINI		GEORGE II LEADS BRITISH ARMY TO VICTORY OVER FRENCH AT DETTINGEN
♩ ♫ ♪		THE CLASSICAL PERIOD	♩ ♫ ♪
1750	ANTONIO SALIERI	TOMASO GIOVANNI ALBINONI JOHANN SEBASTIAN BACH	MINOR EARTHQUAKE IN LONDON
1756	WOLFGANG AMADEUS MOZART		SEVEN YEARS WAR BEGINS
1757		DOMENICO SCARLATTI	CLIVE CONQUERS BENGAL
1759		GEORGE FRIDERIC HANDEL	JAMES BRINDLEY DESIGNS THE WORSLEY TO MANCHESTER CANAL
1767		GEORG PHILIPP TELEMANN	JAMES COOK SETS OUT ON THE VOYAGE THAT WILL SEE THE DISCOVERY OF AUSTRALIA
1770	LUDWIG VAN BEETHOVEN		JAMES COOK DISCOVERS 'NEW SOUTH WALES'
1782	NICCOLÒ PAGANINI	JOHANN CHRISTIAN BACH	RODNEY VICTORIOUS AT THE BATTTLE OF THE SAINTS, SAVING THE BRITISH WEST INDIES
1784	LOUIS SPOHR		SAMUEL JOHNSON DIES

1786	CARL MARIA VON WEBER		COMMERCIALLY MADE ICE-CREAM FIRST ADVERTISED IN NEW YORK
1787		CHRISTOPH WILLIBALD VON GLUCK	AMERICAN CONSTITUTION DRAFTED AND SIGNED IN PHILADELPHIA
1788		CARL PHILIPP EMANUEL BACH	THE FIRST BRITISH CONVICTS ARE TRANSPORTED TO AUSTRALIA
1791		WOLFGANG AMADEUS MOZART	LOUIS XVI AND MARIE ANTOINETTE FLEE
1792	GIOACHINO ROSSINI		FRANCE BECOMES A REPUBLIC
1797	FRANZ SCHUBERT		NAPOLEON FORCES AUSTRIA TO MAKE PEACE WITH FRANCE
1799		KARL DITTERS VON DITTERSDORF	EGYPTIAN HIEROGLYPHICS UNDERSTOOD THROUGH THE DISCOVERY OF THE ROSETTA STONE
1803	HECTOR BERLIOZ		FRANCE SELLS LOUISIANA TO THE USA
1804	JOHANN STRAUSS SNR MIKHAIL GLINKA		SPAIN DECLARES WAR ON BRITAIN
1805		LUIGI BOCCHERINI	NELSON IS VICTORIOUS AT THE BATTLE OF TRAFALGAR

Year			
1809	FELIX MENDELSSOHN	JOSEPH HAYDN	BRITISH ARE DEFEATED AT THE BATTLE OF CORUNNA
1810	FRÉDÉRIC CHOPIN ROBERT SCHUMANN		ARGENTINA BECOMES INDEPENDENT FROM SPAIN
1811	FRANZ LISZT		GEORGE III OF ENGLAND IS DECLARED INSANE
1813	GIUSEPPE VERDI RICHARD WAGNER		ALLIED FORCES INVADE FRANCE
1819	JACQUES OFFENBACH		SINGAPORE IS FOUNDED
1824	ANTON BRUCKNER BEDŘICH SMETANA		TRADES UNIONS LEGALISED IN BRITAIN
1825	JOHANN STRAUSS JNR	ANTONIO SALIERI	FIRST RAILWAY OPENS FROM STOCKTON TO DARLINGTON
1826		CARL MARIA VON WEBER	MENAI SUSPENSION BRIDGE OPENS
1827		LUDWIG VAN BEETHOVEN	TREATY OF LONDON GUARANTEES GREEK INDEPENDENCE
1828		FRANZ SCHUBERT	RUSSIA AND TURKEY AT WAR
♪ ♫ ♪ 1830 THE ROMANTIC PERIOD ♪ ♫ ♪			
1833	JOHANNES BRAHMS ALEXANDER BORODIN		FACTORY ACT PREVENTS CHILDREN UNDER NINE FROM WORKING IN FACTORIES
1835	CAMILLE SAINT-SAËNS		THE WORD 'SOCIALISM' IS FIRST USED

WHO WAS COMPOSING WHAT WHEN?

1836	Léo Delibes		Texas is granted independence from Mexico
1838	Georges Bizet Max Bruch		National Gallery moves to London's Trafalgar Square
1839	Modest Mussorgsky		Britain and Afghanistan at war
1840	Pyotr Ilyich Tchaikovsky	Niccolò Paganini	Penny postage is introduced in Britain
1841	Antonín Dvořák		Britain acquires Hong Kong
1842	Arthur Sullivan		Irish potato famine begins
1843	Edvard Grieg		Natal becomes a British colony
1844	Nikolai Rimsky-Korsakov		First message is sent in Morse code
1845	Gabriel Fauré		Texas joins the USA
1847		Felix Mendelssohn	The British Museum opens
1849		Johann Strauss Snr Frédéric Chopin	Punjab is annnexed by Britain
1856		Robert Schumann	Livingstone completes journey across Africa
1857	Edward Elgar	Mikhail Glinka	Indian Mutiny
1858	Giacomo Puccini		Great Eastern is launched

1859		LOUIS SPOHR	DARWIN PUBLISHES ON THE ORIGIN OF SPECIES
1860	GUSTAV MAHLER ISAAC ALBÉNIZ		ANGLO-CHINESE WAR ENDS
1862	FREDERICK DELIUS CLAUDE DEBUSSY		COTTON FAMINE IN LANCASHIRE
1864	RICHARD STRAUSS		KARL MARX FOUNDS FIRST INTERNATIONAL IN LONDON
1865	JEAN SIBELIUS		WILLIAM BOOTH FOUNDS SALVATION ARMY
1866	ERIK SATIE		AUSTRO-PRUSSIAN WAR ENDS
1868		GIOACHINO ROSSINI	DISRAELI BECOMES PRIME MINISTER IN BRITAIN, BUT IS DEFEATED BY GLADSTONE IN ELECTION
1869		HECTOR BERLIOZ	SUEZ CANAL FORMALLY OPENS
1872	RALPH VAUGHAN WILLIAMS		SECRET BALLOT IS INTRODUCED IN BRITAIN
1873	SERGEI RACHMANINOV		SPAIN BECOMES A REPUBLIC
1874	GUSTAV HOLST ARNOLD SCHOENBERG		SPAIN STOPS BEING A REPUBLIC
1875	MAURICE RAVEL	GEORGES BIZET	BRITAIN BUYS SHARES IN THE SUEZ CANAL

WHO WAS COMPOSING WHAT WHEN?

1880		JACQUES OFFENBACH	BOER REVOLT AGAINST BRITISH IN SOUTH AFRICA
1881	BÉLA BARTÓK	MODEST MUSSORGSKY	PASTEUR PROVES ANIMALS CAN BE IMMUNISED AGAINST ANTHRAX
1882	IGOR STRAVINSKY		CAIRO IS OCCUPIED BY BRITISH TROOPS
1883		RICHARD WAGNER	GERMANY INTRODUCES NATIONAL INSURANCE
1884		BEDŘICH SMETANA	GREENWICH MERIDIAN IS RECOGNISED AS PRIME MERIDIAN
1886		FRANZ LISZT	DAIMLER PRODUCES HIS FIRST MOTOR CAR
1887		ALEXANDER BORODIN	QUEEN VICTORIA CELEBRATES JUBILEE
1891	SERGEI PROKOFIEV	LÉO DELIBES	UNITED STATES OF BRAZIL CREATED
1893		PYOTR ILYICH TCHAIKOVSKY	IRISH HOME RULE BILL DEFEATED BY HOUSE OF LORDS
1896		ANTON BRUCKNER	GOLD DISCOVERED IN THE KLONDIKE
1897		JOHANNES BRAHMS	GREAT GOLD RUSH BEGINS
1898	GEORGE GERSHWIN		THE CURIES DISCOVER RADIUM
1899	FRANCIS POULENC	JOHANN STRAUSS JNR	BOER WAR BEGINS

1900	AARON COPLAND	ARTHUR SULLIVAN	AUSTRALIAN COMMONWEALTH IS PROCLAIMED
1901	JOAQUÍN RODRIGO	GIUSEPPE VERDI	TRANS-SIBERIAN RAILWAY OPENS
1902	WILLIAM WALTON		BOER WAR ENDS
1904		ANTONÍN DVOŘÁK	ENTENTE CORDIALE BETWEEN BRITAIN AND FRANCE
1906	DMITRI SHOSTAKOVICH		VITAMINS DISCOVERED BY F. G. HOPKINS
1907		EDVARD GRIEG	ENTENTE CORDIALE BETWEEN BRITAIN AND RUSSIA
1908		NIKOLAI RIMSKY-KORSAKOV	ASQUITH BECOMES BRITISH PRIME MINISTER
1909		ISAAC ALBÉNIZ	HENRY FORD BEGINS 'ASSEMBLY LINE' PRODUCTION OF CARS

♩ THE ERA OF 20TH AND 21ST CENTURY COMPOSERS ♪

1910	SAMUEL BARBER		FLORENCE NIGHTINGALE DIES
1911		GUSTAV MAHLER	NATIONAL INSURANCE IS INTRODUCED IN BRITAIN
1912	JOHN CAGE		TITANIC SINKS
1913	BENJAMIN BRITTEN		THIRD IRISH HOME RULE BILL PASSES HOUSE OF COMMONS
1918	LEONARD BERNSTEIN	CLAUDE DEBUSSY	WOMEN OVER 30 GET THE VOTE IN BRITAIN

1920		MAX BRUCH	DEGREES FIRST OPEN TO WOMEN AT OXFORD UNIVERSITY
1921		CAMILLE SAINT-SAËNS	IRISH FREE STATE IS ESTABLISHED
1924		GIACOMO PUCCINI GABRIEL FAURÉ	FIRST LABOUR GOVERNMENT IN BRITAIN
1925		ERIK SATIE	SUMMER TIME ACT MADE PERMANENT
1932	JOHN WILLIAMS		SYDNEY HARBOUR BRIDGE OPENS
1933	HENRYK GÓRECKI JOHN BARRY		PROHIBITION ENDS IN THE USA
1934	PETER MAXWELL DAVIES	EDWARD ELGAR FREDERICK DELIUS GUSTAV HOLST	HITLER BECOMES GERMAN DICTATOR
1935	ARVO PÄRT		HITLER ANNOUNCES REARMAMENT OF GERMAN FORCES
1937	PHILIP GLASS	MAURICE RAVEL GEORGE GERSHWIN	BRITISH COALITION GOVERNMENT FORMED UNDER NEVILLE CHAMBERLAIN
1942	PAUL MCCARTNEY		FIRST CONTROLLED NUCLEAR CHAIN REACTION IN URANIUM
1943		SERGEI RACHMANINOV	GERMAN FORCES AT STALINGRAD SURRENDER
1944	JOHN TAVENER KARL JENKINS		FIRST V-2 MISSILE FALLS ON ENGLAND

1945	JOHN RUTTER	BÉLA BARTÓK	WORLD WAR II ENDS
1946	HOWARD SHORE		AMERICANS TEST ATOM BOMB AT BIKINI
1949		RICHARD STRAUSS	CHAIRMAN MAO ZEDONG PROCLAIMS PEOPLE'S REPUBLIC OF CHINA
1951		ARNOLD SCHOENBERG	SIR WINSTON CHURCHILL BECOMES BRITISH PRIME MINISTER FOR THE SECOND TIME
1953	JAMES HORNER	SERGEI PROKOFIEV	HILARY AND TENSING CLIMB MOUNT EVEREST
1955	LUDOVICO EINAUDI		SIR WINSTON CHURCHILL RESIGNS, TO BE REPLACED BY SIR ANTHONY EDEN
1957	HANS ZIMMER	JEAN SIBELIUS	UK'S FIRST HYDROGEN BOMB TEST
1958	HOWARD GOODALL PATRICK HAWES	RALPH VAUGHAN WILLIAMS	GATWICK AIRPORT OPENS
1963		FRANCIS POULENC	£2.6M STOLEN IN BRITISH 'GREAT TRAIN ROBBERY'
1971	JOBY TALBOT	IGOR STRAVINSKY	BRITISH EDUCATION SECRETARY MARGARET THATCHER ANNOUNCES END OF FREE SCHOOL MILK
1975	PAUL MEALOR	DMITRI SHOSTAKOVICH	UK VOTES IN REFERENDUM TO JOIN THE EUROPEAN COMMUNITY

WHO WAS COMPOSING WHAT WHEN?

1976		BENJAMIN BRITTEN	JAMES CALLAGHAN BECOMES BRITISH PRIME MINISTER
1981		SAMUEL BARBER	PRESIDENT REAGAN SHOT IN WASHINGTON
1983		WILLIAM WALTON	FIRST UK HEART–LUNG TRANSPLANT
1990		AARON COPLAND LEONARD BERNSTEIN	NELSON MANDELA IS FREED AFTER 25 YEARS IN JAIL
1992		JOHN CAGE	CLASSIC FM BEGINS BROADCASTING
1999		JOAQUÍN RODRIGO	YEHUDI MENUHIN DIES
2010		HENRYK GÓRECKI	THE CONSERVATIVES AND LIBERAL DEMOCRATS FORM BRITAIN'S FIRST POST-WAR COALITION GOVERNMENT
2011		JOHN BARRY	PRINCE WILLIAM AND CATHERINE MIDDLETON MARRY, BECOMING THE DUKE AND DUCHESS OF CAMBRIDGE
2012			CLASSIC FM CELEBRATES ITS 20TH BIRTHDAY

CHAPTER 11

THE CLASSIC FM HALL OF FAME TOP 300

We first launched the Classic FM Hall of Fame back in 1996. We had no idea back then that we were giving birth to a phenomenon. It has become so much more than just an annual chart – spawning a daily radio programme, a whole series of bestselling CDs and even *The Classic FM Hall of Fame* book, which appeared in the *Sunday Times* bestsellers list in 2011.

Since we started our quest to identify the United Kingdom's favourite pieces of classical music, we have produced 16 separate annual charts. Each one offers a snapshot of our listeners' favourites at a given point in time. We are often asked how we go about compiling the chart. What happens is that, at the beginning of each year, we ask our listeners to send us their top three all-time classical favourites. Every single one of those votes is registered on a computer, which creates a running tally of the relative positions of each of the pieces. The final chart is produced just before Easter. Classic FM's team of music producers then sets about the unenviable task of fitting all 300 works into one 48-hour countdown, which is broadcast from dawn to dusk on Good Friday, Easter Saturday, Easter Sunday and Easter Monday.

The chart we have included here is a distillation of all of those 16 years of charts, which we broadcast in full at the beginning of 2012. How did we arrive at this 'ultimate' Classic FM Hall of Fame? Well, we took the annual Top 300 from 1996 to 2011 and created a new Top 300 based on each work's relative position in the annual countdowns. That means that all of the works that have seen their popularity ebb and flow over the decade and a half since the Classic FM Hall of Fame began receive a chart position based on an aggregation of their positions over the full period. New works entering the chart in more recent years (in many cases because they hadn't actually been composed as far back as 1996) are more likely to appear further down our chart because they don't benefit from listeners' votes in the early years of the countdown.

The Classic FM Hall of Fame is very much a living, breathing entity, reflecting fashions and events in the world around us. For this reason, there can never be a single definitive chart – only a series of snapshots of tastes at any given moment in time. Each year the chart changes, so who knows which composers will come to the fore, which film scores and operas will capture our collective imagination, or which long-forgotten pieces will be revitalised by a new recording.

1	RACHMANINOV	PIANO CONCERTO NO. 2
2	MOZART	CLARINET CONCERTO
3	BRUCH	VIOLIN CONCERTO NO. 1
4	VAUGHAN WILLIAMS	THE LARK ASCENDING
5	BEETHOVEN	PIANO CONCERTO NO. 5 ('EMPEROR')
6	ELGAR	CELLO CONCERTO IN E MINOR
7	BEETHOVEN	SYMPHONY NO. 6 ('PASTORAL')
8	ELGAR	ENIGMA VARIATIONS
9	BEETHOVEN	SYMPHONY NO. 9 ('ODE TO JOY')
10	PACHELBEL	CANON IN D
11	BARBER	ADAGIO FOR STRINGS
12	GRIEG	PIANO CONCERTO IN A MINOR
13	VAUGHAN WILLIAMS	FANTASIA ON A THEME BY THOMAS TALLIS

14	SAINT-SÄENS	SYMPHONY NO. 3 ('ORGAN')
15	HOLST	THE PLANETS
16	BIZET	THE PEARL FISHERS
17	HANDEL	MESSIAH
18	DVOŘÁK	SYMPHONY NO. 9 ('FROM THE NEW WORLD')
19	MOZART	REQUIEM
20	VIVALDI	FOUR SEASONS
21	ALLEGRI	MISERERE
22	RACHMANINOV	SYMPHONY NO. 2
23	RODRIGO	CONCIERTO DE ARANJUEZ
24	MASCAGNI	CAVALLERIA RUSTICANA
25	FAURÉ	REQUIEM
26	SIBELIUS	FINLANDIA
27	MENDELSSOHN	VIOLIN CONCERTO
28	MOZART	PIANO CONCERTO NO. 21
29	BEETHOVEN	SYMPHONY NO. 7
30	MAHLER	SYMPHONY NO. 5
31	RACHMANINOV	RHAPSODY ON A THEME OF PAGANINI
32	BEETHOVEN	SYMPHONY NO. 5
33	J. S. BACH	DOUBLE VIOLIN CONCERTO
34	TCHAIKOVSKY	1812 OVERTURE
35	RIMSKY-KORSAKOV	SCHEHERAZADE
36	RACHMANINOV	PIANO CONCERTO NO. 3
37	BEETHOVEN	PIANO SONATA NO. 14 ('MOONLIGHT')
38	TCHAIKOVSKY	PIANO CONCERTO NO. 1
39	SHOSTAKOVICH	PIANO CONCERTO NO. 2
40	BEETHOVEN	VIOLIN CONCERTO

41	ALBINONI	ADAGIO IN G MINOR
42	FAURÉ	CANTIQUE DE JEAN RACINE
43	SMETANA	MÁ VLAST (INCLUDING VLTAVA)
44	GERSHWIN	RHAPSODY IN BLUE
45	TCHAIKOVSKY	SYMPHONY NO. 6 ('PATHÉTIQUE')
46	PROKOFIEV	ROMEO AND JULIET
47	SHOSTAKOVICH	THE GADFLY
48	J. S. BACH	TOCCATA AND FUGUE IN D MINOR
49	MOZART	THE MARRIAGE OF FIGARO
50	VERDI	NABUCCO
51	CHOPIN	PIANO CONCERTO NO. 1
52	GRIEG	PEER GYNT SUITE NO. 1
53	ORFF	CARMINA BURANA
54	J. S. BACH	BRANDENBURG CONCERTOS
55	HANDEL	SOLOMON
56	VERDI	REQUIEM
57	TCHAIKOVSKY	SWAN LAKE
58	WIDOR	ORGAN SYMPHONY NO. 5
59	HANDEL	ZADOK THE PRIEST
60	RICHARD STRAUSS	FOUR LAST SONGS
61	PUCCINI	MADAMA BUTTERFLY
62	MENDELSSOHN	HEBRIDES OVERTURE ('FINGAL'S CAVE')
63	MOZART	THE MAGIC FLUTE
64	DEBUSSY	SUITE BERGAMASQUE (INCLUDES 'CLAIR DE LUNE')
65	CHOPIN	PIANO CONCERTO NO. 2
66	SCHUBERT	PIANO QUINTET IN A ('TROUT')
67	MOZART	FLUTE AND HARP CONCERTO

68	PUCCINI	*LA BOHÈME*
69	MOZART	*AVE VERUM CORPUS*
70	SIBELIUS	*SYMPHONY NO. 5*
71	MASSENET	*THAÏS (INCLUDES 'MEDITATION')*
72	MOZART	*SOLEMN VESPERS*
73	BEETHOVEN	*SYMPHONY NO. 3 ('EROICA')*
74	MOZART	*EINE KLEINE NACHTMUSIK*
75	MAHLER	*SYMPHONY NO. 2 ('RESURRECTION')*
76	TCHAIKOVSKY	*SYMPHONY NO. 5*
77	SIBELIUS	*KARELIA SUITE*
78	J. S. BACH	*ST MATTHEW PASSION*
79	KHACHATURIAN	*SPARTACUS*
80	RAVEL	*BOLÉRO*
81	SIBELIUS	*SYMPHONY NO. 2*
82	TCHAIKOVSKY	*VIOLIN CONCERTO IN D*
83	BRAHMS	*VIOLIN CONCERTO IN D*
84	SIBELIUS	*VIOLIN CONCERTO IN D MINOR*
85	JOHANN STRAUSS JNR	*BY THE BEAUTIFUL BLUE DANUBE*
86	UNGAR	*THE ASHOKAN FAREWELL*
87	TCHAIKOVSKY	*THE NUTCRACKER*
88	J. S. BACH	*MASS IN B MINOR*
89	VERDI	*LA TRAVIATA*
90	MUSSORGSKY	*PICTURES AT AN EXHIBITION*
91	ELGAR	*THE DREAM OF GERONTIUS*
92	WAGNER	*TANNHÄUSER*
93	WAGNER	*DIE WALKÜRE*
94	WAGNER	*TRISTAN AND ISOLDE*

95	DELIBES	LAKMÉ
96	VERDI	AIDA
97	SCHUBERT	STRING QUINTET IN C, D. 956
98	GÓRECKI	SYMPHONY NO. 3 ('SYMPHONY OF SORROWFUL SONGS')
99	BIZET	CARMEN
100	ELGAR	POMP AND CIRCUMSTANCE MARCHES
101	TALLIS	SPEM IN ALIUM
102	HANDEL	WATER MUSIC SUITE NO. 1
103	DVOŘÁK	CELLO CONCERTO IN B MINOR
104	BUTTERWORTH	THE BANKS OF GREEN WILLOW
105	FAURÉ	PAVANE
106	TCHAIKOVSKY	ROMEO AND JULIET
107	SAINT-SAËNS	CARNIVAL OF THE ANIMALS
108	MOZART	COSÌ FAN TUTTE
109	SAINT-SAËNS	DANSE MACABRE
110	BRAHMS	A GERMAN REQUIEM
111	JENKINS	THE ARMED MAN (A MASS FOR PEACE)
112	BEETHOVEN	ROMANCE NO. 2
113	BACH	CANTATA BWV 147: 'JESU JOY OF MAN'S DESIRING'
114	BERLIOZ	SYMPHONIE FANTASTIQUE
115	VIVALDI	GLORIA IN D
116	MOZART	CLARINET QUINTET
117	COPLAND	APPALACHIAN SPRING
118	BRUCH	SCOTTISH FANTASY
119	WILLIAMS	SCHINDLER'S LIST

120	BEETHOVEN	PIANO CONCERTO NO. 4
121	SHORE	LORD OF THE RINGS
122	SATIE	GYMNOPÉDIES
123	BEETHOVEN	PIANO SONATA NO. 8 ('PATHÉTIQUE')
124	EINAUDI	LE ONDE
125	TCHAIKOVSKY	SLEEPING BEAUTY
126	BORODIN	IN THE STEPPES OF CENTRAL ASIA
127	GRIEG	HOLBERG SUITE
128	DVOŘÁK	RUSALKA
129	VAUGHAN WILLIAMS	FANTASIA ON GREENSLEEVES
130	PÄRT	SPIEGEL IM SPIEGEL
131	J. S. BACH	CELLO SUITES
132	MOZART	SYMPHONY NO. 40
133	BRAHMS	PIANO CONCERTO NO. 2
134	VAUGHAN WILLIAMS	5 VARIANTS OF DIVES AND LAZARUS
135	SCHUBERT	SYMPHONY NO. 9 ('GREAT')
136	GOUNOD	MORS ET VITA
137	PUCCINI	TOSCA
138	COPLAND	FANFARE FOR THE COMMON MAN
139	MENDELSSOHN	SYMPHONY NO. 4 ('ITALIAN')
140	BORODIN	PRINCE IGOR
141	BARBER	VIOLIN CONCERTO
142	JENKINS	ADIEMUS
143	J. S. BACH	ORCHESTRAL SUITE NO. 3
144	VIVALDI	MANDOLIN CONCERTO, RV425
145	TCHAIKOVSKY	SYMPHONY NO. 4
146	GLASS	VIOLIN CONCERTO

147	MOZART	PIANO CONCERTO NO. 23
148	ROSSINI	WILLIAM TELL
149	STRAVINSKY	THE RITE OF SPRING
150	ROSSINI	THE THIEVING MAGPIE
151	SHOSTAKOVICH	SYMPHONY NO. 5
152	J. S. BACH	GOLDBERG VARIATIONS
153	HANDEL	XERXES
154	MOZART	PIANO CONCERTO NO. 20
155	MENDELSSOHN	A MIDSUMMER NIGHT'S DREAM
156	HANDEL	MUSIC FOR THE ROYAL FIREWORKS
157	SHOSTAKOVICH	JAZZ SUITE NO. 2
158	PUCCINI	TURANDOT
159	MOZART	DON GIOVANNI
160	WILLIAMS	STAR WARS
161	MORRICONE	THE MISSION (INCLUDES 'GABRIEL'S OBOE')
162	DEBUSSY	PRÉLUDE À L'APRÈS-MIDI D'UN FAUNE
163	SHOSTAKOVICH	JAZZ SUITE NO. 1
164	BEETHOVEN	EGMONT OVERTURE
165	SAINT-SAËNS	SAMSON AND DELILA
166	HAYDN	THE CREATION
167	LITOLFF	CONCERTO SYMPHONIQUE NO. 4
168	MOZART	HORN CONCERTO NO. 4
169	VIVALDI	MOTET IN E, RV630
170	CANTELOUBE	SONGS OF THE AUVERGNE
171	MOZART	SYMPHONY NO. 41 ('JUPITER')
172	BELLINI	NORMA
173	HAYDN	TRUMPET CONCERTO IN E FLAT

174	SCHUBERT	SYMPHONY NO. 5
175	TCHAIKOVSKY	CAPRICCIO ITALIEN
176	MAHLER	SYMPHONY NO. 1 ('TITAN')
177	BEETHOVEN	BAGATELLE NO. 25 ('FÜR ELISE')
178	ZIPOLI	ELEVAZIONE
179	ELGAR	VIOLIN CONCERTO
180	SCHUMANN	PIANO CONCERTO
181	GLUCK	ORFEO AND EURIDICE
182	PUCCINI	GIANNI SCHICCHI
183	TARREGA	RECUERDOS DE LA ALHAMBRA
184	VAUGHAN WILLIAMS	ENGLISH FOLKSONGS SUITE
185	WILLIAMS	HARRY POTTER
186	ADDINSELL	WARSAW CONCERTO
187	RUTTER	REQUIEM
188	SCHUBERT	SYMPHONY NO. 8 ('UNFINISHED')
189	ZIMMER	GLADIATOR
190	JOHANN STRAUSS SNR	RADETZKY MARCH
191	BRAHMS	SYMPHONY NO. 4
192	HANDEL	SARABANDE
193	WAGNER	SIEGFRIED
194	WALTON	CROWN IMPERIAL
195	ELGAR	SYMPHONY NO. 1
196	WAGNER	LOHENGRIN
197	ELGAR	CHANSON DE MATIN
198	PAGANINI	VIOLIN CONCERTO NO. 1
199	BEETHOVEN	PIANO CONCERTO NO. 3
200	MACCUNN	THE LAND OF THE MOUNTAIN AND THE FLOOD

201	PROKOFIEV	SYMPHONY NO. 1 ('CLASSICAL')
202	BORODIN	STRING QUARTET NO. 2
203	MAXWELL DAVIES	FAREWELL TO STROMNESS
204	ELGAR	INTRODUCTION AND ALLEGRO FOR STRINGS
205	STRAVINSKY	THE FIREBIRD
206	PURCELL	DIDO AND AENEAS
207	DVOŘÁK	SYMPHONY NO. 8
208	SHOSTAKOVICH	THE UNFORGETTABLE YEAR 1919
209	WILLIAMS	SAVING PRIVATE RYAN
210	FINZI	ECLOGUE
211	RAVEL	PAVANE POUR UNE INFANTE DÉFUNTE
212	RICHARD STRAUSS	DER ROSENKAVALIER
213	BEETHOVEN	PIANO CONCERTO NO. 1
214	DELIUS	A VILLAGE ROMEO AND JULIET
215	BRAHMS	SYMPHONY NO. 1
216	BEETHOVEN	TRIPLE CONCERTO
217	ALBINONI	OBOE CONCERTO IN D MINOR, OP. 9 NO. 2
218	MONTEVERDI	VESPERS
219	WAGNER	THE MASTERSINGERS OF NUREMBERG
220	EINAUDI	I GIORNI
221	J. S. BACH	CANTATA BWV 208: 'SHEEP MAY SAFELY GRAZE'
222	BRAHMS	PIANO CONCERTO NO. 1
223	MAHLER	SYMPHONY NO. 8 ('SYMPHONY OF A THOUSAND')
224	HAWES	QUANTA QUALIA
225	MUSSORGSKY	NIGHT ON THE BARE MOUNTAIN
226	WAGNER	GÖTTERDÄMMERUNG
227	BEETHOVEN	FANTASIA FOR PIANO, CHORUS AND ORCHESTRA

228	ELGAR	SERENADE FOR STRINGS
229	CHOPIN	NOCTURNE, OP. 9 NO. 2
230	RACHMANINOV	PIANO CONCERTO NO. 1
231	VAUGHAN WILLIAMS	THE WASPS OVERTURE
232	VERDI	RIGOLETTO
233	SIBELIUS	THE SWAN OF TUONELA
234	BRAHMS	SYMPHONY NO. 3
235	LISZT	HUNGARIAN RHAPSODIES
236	BRITTEN	PETER GRIMES
237	BRUCH	KOL NIDREI
238	ELGAR	SALUT D'AMOUR
239	GOUNOD	ST CECILIA MASS
240	VIVALDI	CHAMBER CONCERTO IN D FOR LUTE
241	DELIUS	LA CALINDA
242	HESS	LADIES IN LAVENDER
243	TAVENER	SONG FOR ATHENE
244	ROSSINI	THE BARBER OF SEVILLE
245	MOZART	SINFONIA CONCERTANTE FOR VIOLIN AND VIOLA
246	ELGAR	SEA PICTURES
247	FRANCK	PANIS ANGELICUS
248	BARRY	DANCES WITH WOLVES
249	PERGOLESI	STABAT MATER
250	MOZART	EXSULTATE JUBILATE
251	MAHLER	SYMPHONY NO. 4
252	JENKINS	REQUIEM
253	JENKINS	PALLADIO
254	KHACHATURIAN	MASQUERADE SUITE

255	PREISNER	*REQUIEM FOR MY FRIEND*
256	SCHUBERT	*AVE MARIA*
257	STANLEY	*TRUMPET VOLUNTARY*
258	J. S. BACH	*CANTATA NO. 140: 'WACHET AUF'*
259	PARRY	*I WAS GLAD*
260	JOHANN STRAUSS JNR	*DIE FLEDERMAUS*
261	RUTTER	*A GAELIC BLESSING*
262	PARRY	*JERUSALEM*
263	GERSHWIN	*PIANO CONCERTO*
264	BRUCH	*VIOLIN CONCERTO NO. 2*
265	RACHMANINOV	*VESPERS*
266	RAVEL	*PIANO CONCERTO*
267	OFFENBACH	*THE TALES OF HOFFMANN*
268	CACCINI	*AVE MARIA*
269	GRIEG	*LYRIC PIECES*
270	BERLIOZ	*L'ENFANCE DU CHRIST*
271	COPLAND	*RODEO*
272	BRAHMS	*SYMPHONY NO. 2*
273	VAUGHAN WILLIAMS	*SYMPHONY NO. 1 ('A SEA SYMPHONY')*
274	DVOŘÁK	*SLAVONIC DANCES*
275	MENDELSSOHN	*ELIJAH*
276	MOZART	*MASS NO. 18 ('GREAT')*
277	WALTON	*SPITFIRE PRELUDE AND FUGUE*
278	VAUGHAN	*WILLIAMS SYMPHONY NO. 5*
279	LAURIDSEN	*O MAGNUM MYSTERIUM*
280	LORD DURHAM	*CONCERTO*
281	DELIUS	*ON HEARING THE FIRST CUCKOO IN SPRING*

282	BARRY	THE BEYONDNESS OF THINGS
283	PROKOFIEV	LIEUTENANT KIJÉ
284	MCCARTNEY	STANDING STONE
285	VAUGHAN WILLIAMS	SYMPHONY NO. 2 ('A LONDON SYMPHONY')
286	HORNER	TITANIC
287	TCHAIKOVSKY	PIANO CONCERTO NO. 2
288	DELIBES	COPPÉLIA
289	LEHÁR	THE MERRY WIDOW
290	SCHUBERT	IMPROMPTU NO. 3
291	RAMEAU	LES INDES GALANTES
292	HUMMEL	TRUMPET CONCERTO
293	BERNSTEIN	CANDIDE
294	TCHAIKOVSKY	SERENADE FOR STRINGS
295	DONIZETTI	LUCIA DI LAMMERMOOR
296	VIVALDI	DOUBLE CONCERTO FOR TWO MANDOLINS, RV532
297	BARRY	OUT OF AFRICA
298	RODRIGO	FANTASIA PARA UN GENTILHOMBRE
299	HAYDN	CELLO CONCERTO NO. 1
300	VERDI	LA FORZA DEL DESTINO

CHAPTER 12

WHAT THEY SAID ABOUT EACH OTHER

They might have been creative geniuses, but the great composers and performers never held back when it came to sparing the feelings of their colleagues, as shown in this selection of sayings from some of the stars of the classical music world:

Rossini would have been a great composer if his teacher had spanked him enough on the backside.

Ludwig van Beethoven, composer

I played over the music of that scoundrel Brahms. What a giftless bastard! It annoys me that his self-inflated mediocrity is hailed as genius.

Pyotr Ilyich Tchaikovsky, composer

On Hector Berlioz's *Symphonie fantastique*:

What a good thing it isn't music.
Gioachino Rossini, composer

Also about Hector Berlioz:

One ought to wash one's hands after dealing with one of his scores.
Felix Mendelssohn, composer

I'm told that Saint-Saëns has informed a delighted public that since war began he has composed music for the stage, melodies, an elegy and a piece for the trombone. If he'd been making shellcases instead it might have been all the better for music.
Maurice Ravel, composer

Listening to the Fifth Symphony of Ralph Vaughan Williams is like staring at a cow for 45 minutes.
Aaron Copland, composer

On hearing John Cage's 4'33", which comprises no music, just four and a half minutes of silence:

I look forward to hearing his longer works.
Igor Stravinsky, composer

Wagner has lovely moments but awful quarters of an hour.
Gioachino Rossini, composer

One can't judge Wagner's opera Lohengrin *after a first hearing, and I certainly don't intend hearing it a second time.*
Gioacchino Rossini, composer

Too many pieces finish too long after the end.
Igor Stravinsky, composer

Modern music is as dangerous as cocaine.
Pietro Mascagni, composer

I occasionally play works by contemporary composers, and for two reasons. First, to discourage the composer from writing any more, and secondly to remind myself how much I appreciate Beethoven.

Jascha Heifetz, violinist

About Claude Debussy's *La Mer*:

The audience ... expected the ocean, something colossal, but they were served instead with some agitated water in a saucer.

Louis Schneider, composer

Also about Debussy:

Debussy is like a painter who looks at his canvas to see what more he can take out. Strauss is like a painter who has covered every inch and then takes the paint he has left and throws it at the canvas.

Ernest Bloch, composer

To a violinist who believed that a passage was impossible to play:

When I composed that, I was conscious of being inspired by God Almighty. Do you think I consider your puny little fiddle when He speaks to me?

Ludwig van Beethoven, composer

I am not interested in having an orchestra sound like itself. I want it to sound like the composer.

Leonard Bernstein, conductor and composer

After hearing an opera by another composer:

I like your opera – I think I will set it to music.

Ludwig van Beethoven, composer

CHAPTER 13

CLASSICAL MUSIC USED IN FILMS

Classical music and the cinema have been inextricably linked since the earliest days of film.

Today, many contemporary composers have made their names through their film soundtrack work, as we discovered in Chapter 9. However, movie directors have never just limited themselves to commissioning new music when much of the old stuff adds drama or evokes an emotion in a particular scene. So much classical music is used in films that it has become one of the easiest ways for people to listen to classical music without even realising it.

So, if you are planning to indoctrinate someone you know in the ways of all things classical, you could do worse than buying the DVDs or downloading from iTunes a few of the films featured on this list:

FILM	COMPOSER	WORK
2000 LEAGUES UNDER THE SEA	J. S. BACH	TOCCATA AND FUGUE IN D MINOR
2001: A SPACE ODYSSEY	RICHARD STRAUSS	ALSO SPRACH ZARATHUSTRA
ACE VENTURA: PET DETECTIVE	MOZART	EINE KLEINE NACHTMUSIK

AN AMERICAN WEREWOLF IN LONDON	RAVEL	*DAPHNIS AND CHLOE*
APOCALYPSE NOW	WAGNER	*RIDE OF THE VALKYRIES*
AS GOOD AS IT GETS	GERSHWIN	*AN AMERICAN IN PARIS*
AUSTIN POWERS	JOHANN STRAUSS SNR	*BY THE BEAUTIFUL BLUE DANUBE*
BABE	SAINT-SAËNS	*SYMPHONY NO. 3*
A BEAUTIFUL MIND	MOZART	*PIANO SONATA NO. 11*
BEND IT LIKE BECKHAM	PUCCINI	*'NESSUN DORMA' FROM TURANDOT*
BILLY ELLIOT	TCHAIKOVSKY	*SWAN LAKE*
BRASSED OFF	RODRIGO	*CONCIERTO DE ARANJUEZ*
BRIDGET JONES'S DIARY	HANDEL	*'HALLELUJAH CHORUS' FROM MESSIAH*
CAPTAIN CORELLI'S MANDOLIN	PUCCINI	*'O MIO BABBINO CARO' FROM GIANNI SCHICCHI*
CATCH ME IF YOU CAN	HAYDN	*PIANO CONCERTO NO. 11*
CHARIOTS OF FIRE	ALLEGRI	*MISERERE*
A CLOCKWORK ORANGE	BEETHOVEN	*SYMPHONY NO. 9*
DEAD POETS SOCIETY	BEETHOVEN	*PIANO CONCERTO NO. 5*
DRIVING MISS DAISY	DVOŘÁK	*'SONG TO THE MOON' FROM RUSALKA*
THE ELEPHANT MAN	BARBER	*ADAGIO FOR STRINGS*
THE ENGLISH PATIENT	J. S. BACH	*'ARIA' FROM GOLDBERG VARIATIONS*
FOUR WEDDINGS AND A FUNERAL	HANDEL	*ARRIVAL OF THE QUEEN OF SHEBA*
THE FRENCH LIEUTENANT'S WOMAN	MOZART	*PIANO SONATA NO. 15*

THE HORSE WHISPERER	BEETHOVEN	CELLO SONATA NO. 1
INDECENT PROPOSAL	VIVALDI	CONCERTO NO. 8 FROM L'ESTRO ARMONICO
JFK	MOZART	HORN CONCERTO NO. 2
JOHNNY ENGLISH	HANDEL	ZADOK THE PRIEST
L.A. CONFIDENTIAL	MENDELS-SOHN	HEBRIDES OVERTURE
THE LADYKILLERS	BOCCHERINI	MINUET
LARA CROFT: TOMB RAIDER	J. S. BACH	KEYBOARD CONCERTO NO. 5 IN F MINOR
MONA LISA	PUCCINI	'LOVE DUET' FROM MADAMA BUTTERFLY
MR HOLLAND'S OPUS	BEETHOVEN	SYMPHONY NO. 7
MRS DOUBTFIRE	ROSSINI	'LARGO AL FACTOTUM' FROM THE BARBER OF SEVILLE
MY BIG FAT GREEK WEDDING	WAGNER	'BRIDAL CHORUS' FROM LOHENGRIN
MY LEFT FOOT	SCHUBERT	'TROUT' QUINTET
NATURAL BORN KILLERS	ORFF	CARMINA BURANA
OCEAN'S ELEVEN	DEBUSSY	CLAIR DE LUNE
OUT OF AFRICA	MOZART	CLARINET CONCERTO
PHILADELPHIA	MOZART	'LAUDATE DOMINUM'
PLATOON	BARBER	ADAGIO FOR STRINGS
PRETTY WOMAN	VIVALDI	FOUR SEASONS
A ROOM WITH A VIEW	PUCCINI	'DORETTA'S DREAM' FROM LA RONDINE

CLASSICAL MUSIC USED IN FILMS

THE SHAWSHANK REDEMPTION	MOZART	*'CHE SOAVE ZEFFIRETTO'* FROM *THE MARRIAGE OF FIGARO*
SHERLOCK HOLMES: A GAME OF SHADOWS	SCHUBERT	*'DIE FORELLE'*
THE SILENCE OF THE LAMBS	J. S. BACH	*GOLDBERG VARIATIONS*
SLEEPING WITH THE ENEMY	BERLIOZ	*SYMPHONIE FANTASTIQUE*
THE TALENTED MR RIPLEY	J. S. BACH	*ITALIAN CONCERTO*
THERE'S SOMETHING ABOUT MARY	BIZET	*'DANSE BOHÉMIENNE'* FROM *CARMEN*
TOY STORY 2	RICHARD STRAUSS	*ALSO SPRACH ZARATHUSTRA*
TRAINSPOTTING	BIZET	*'HABANERA'* FROM *CARMEN*
THE TRUMAN SHOW	CHOPIN	*PIANO CONCERTO NO. 1*
WALL STREET	VERDI	*'QUESTA O QUELLA'* FROM *RIGOLETTO*
WAYNE'S WORLD	TCHAIKOVSKY	*ROMEO AND JULIET*
WHO FRAMED ROGER RABBIT?	LISZT	*HUNGARIAN RHAPSODY NO. 2*

CHAPTER 14

WHERE TO FIND OUT MORE

If this book has whetted your appetite to find out more, one of the best ways to discover what you like about classical music is to tune in to Classic FM. We broadcast 24 hours a day across the UK on 100–102 FM, on Digital Radio, online at www.classicfm.com, on Sky Channel 0106, on Virgin Media channel 922 and on FreeSat channel 721. We play a huge breadth of different classical music each week.

As well as being able to listen online, you will find a host of interactive features about classical music, composers and musicians on our website, classicfm.com. When we first turned on Classic FM's transmitters 20 years ago, we changed the face of classical music radio in the UK for ever. Two decades later, we have big plans to do the same online, so you will find that our website will be growing in terms of editorial content and features over the coming months.

If books are more your thing than websites, then we would very much like to recommend the two companion volumes to *Everything You Ever Wanted To Know About Classical Music ... but were too afraid to ask*. Both are published by Elliott & Thompson. The first, *Classic Ephemera*, is a musical miscellany, packed with all manner of handy information: telling trivia, curious quotes and fascinating facts. The second, *The Classic FM Hall of Fame*, profiles the 300 greatest classical works and their composers – as voted by Classic FM listeners.

If you would like to delve far, far deeper into the subject than we have been able to do in this short book, the universally acknowledged authority on the subject is *The New Grove Dictionary of Music and Musicians*. The original version was edited by Sir George Grove, with the eminent musicologist Stanley Sadie taking over the reins for this new edition (published in 1995). But be warned – this is a weighty tome, running to 20 hardback volumes with around 29,000 separate articles.

In truth, this massive resource is far more detailed than most music lovers would ever need; a more manageable reference book is *The Concise Oxford Dictionary of Music*, edited by Michael Kennedy (published by Oxford Reference), or *The Penguin Companion to Classical Music*, edited by Paul Griffiths (published by Penguin). Paul Griffiths has also written *A Concise History of Western Music* (published by Cambridge University Press) – a highly readable discussion of the way in which classical music has evolved over time.

The DK Eyewitness Companion to Classical Music, edited by John Burrows (published by Dorling Kindersley), is a very colourful and reliable source of information on the chronology of classical music. Howard Goodall delves into five episodes that changed musical history, including the invention of musical notation and the creation of the recording industry, in his excellent book *Big Bangs* (published by Vintage). For a slightly quirkier walk through the subject, we recommend *Stephen Fry's Incomplete & Utter History of Classical Music*, which is published by Macmillan and is based on the award-winning Classic FM radio series of the same name, written by Tim Lihoreau.

Other excellent general guides to classical music include: *The Rough Guide to Classical Music*, edited by Joe Staines (published by Rough Guides); *The Encyclopedia of Music* by Max Wade-Matthews and Wendy Thompson (published by Hermes House); *Good Music Guide* by Neville Garden (published by Columbia Marketing); *The Chronical of Classical Music* by Alan Kendall (published by Thames & Hudson); *The Lives & Times of The Great Composers* by Michael Steen (published by Icon); *The Lives of the Great Composers* by Harold C. Schonberg (published by Abacus); and *Music for the People: The Pleasures and Pitfalls of Classical Music* by Gareth Malone, whose television series on singing are fast making him a national treasure (published by Collins). If you ever happen across a copy of either of Jeremy Nicholas's two splendid books, *The Classic FM Guide to Classical Music* (published by Pavilion) and *The Classic FM Good Music Guide* (published by Hodder & Stoughton), then you should snap them up. Both are sadly out of print at the moment.

Three excellent books on the subject of opera are *The DK Eyewitness Guide to Opera* (published by Dorling Kindersley); *The Good Opera Guide* by Denis Forman (published by Phoenix); and *The Rough Guide to Opera* by Matthew Boyden (published by Rough Guides).

For younger classical music lovers or discoverers, *The Story of Classical Music* and *Famous Composers* are both published by Naxos Audiobooks. These titles are aimed at eight-to-fourteen-year-olds and contain musical excerpts and CD-ROM elements.

The very best way of finding out more about which pieces of classical music you like is by going out and hearing a live performance for yourself. There is simply no substitute for seeing the whites of the eyes of a talented soloist as he or she performs a masterpiece on a stage only a few feet in front of you. Before you go, make sure that you read our guide to going to a live classical concert back on pages 34 to 38. Classic FM has a series of partnerships with orchestras across the country: the Royal Scottish National Orchestra, Northern Sinfonia, the Royal Liverpool Philharmonic Orchestra, the Orchestra of Opera North, the Philharmonia Orchestra and the London Symphony Orchestra. To see if they have a concert coming up near you, log onto our website at classicfm.com and click on the 'Concerts and Events' section. It will also include many of the other classical concerts – both professional and amateur – that are taking place near to where you live.

Happy listening!

FOR A COMPLETE LIST OF ALL THE RECORDINGS RECOMMENDED THROUGHOUT THIS BOOK, GO ONLINE TO WWW.CLASSICFM.COM/EVERYTHING.

YOU'LL ALSO FIND LINKS TO DOWNLOAD ALL OF OUR RECOMMENDATIONS FROM iTUNES, AS WELL AS MORE INFORMATION ABOUT *EVERYTHING YOU EVER WANTED TO KNOW ABOUT CLASSICAL MUSIC ... BUT WERE TOO AFRAID TO ASK.*

ACKNOWLEDGEMENTS

Enormous thanks are due to Global Radio's Founder and Executive President, Ashley Tabor, to Group Chief Executive Stephen Miron, to Director of Broadcasting Richard Park and to Chairman Sir Charles Allen, each of whom has given us unstinting encouragement and support.

Among the Classic FM programming team, we must thank Nick Bailey, Jamie Beesley, Fiona Bowden, John Brunning, Stuart Campbell, Chris Chilvers, Lucy Coward, Jamie Crick, Nick Ferrari, Mark Forrest, Howard Goodall, Matt Gubbins, Owen Hopkin, Bob Jones, Jane Jones, Myleene Klass, Tim Lihoreau, Laurence Llewelyn-Bowen, David Mellor, Anne-Marie Minhall, Jenny Nelson, Phil Noyce, Bill Overton, Nicholas Owen, Emma Oxborrow, Alexandra Philpotts, John Suchet, Margherita Taylor, Alan Titchmarsh, Natalie Wheen and Andrew Wright. Thanks also to Matt Rennie, Caeshia St Paul, Giles Pearman, Andrea Flamini, Felix Meston and John Chittenden.

We are incredibly grateful to Lorne Forsyth, Olivia Bays and Nick Sidwell at our publishers Elliott & Thompson for once more guiding and supporting us through the writing of this book with enormous grace, wisdom, enthusiasm and good humour.

The people who work at a radio station are only one half of its story, so 20 years after Classic FM first went on air, we want to say a massive and very deeply heartfelt 'thank you' to all of our millions of listeners. Without your involvement, Classic FM would quite simply never have achieved the successes it has. Here's to the next 20 years of the world's greatest music.

ABOUT THE
AUTHORS

Darren Henley is the Managing Director of Global Radio's national classical music station, Classic FM. The author of 24 books about music and musicians, he studied politics at the University of Hull. He has authored two independent reviews of music and cultural education in England for the Department for Education and the Department for Culture, Media and Sport. He continues to advise ministers on these two areas, as well as chairing the Mayor of London's Music Education Steering Group and the advisory group for the Department for Communities and Local Government's 'Our Big Gig' programme. He is a member of the Scottish Government's Musical Instrument group; a member of the governing body of the Associated Board of the Royal Schools of Music; a Patron of the Mayor of London's Fund for Young Musicians; and a Vice-President of the Canterbury Festival. He sits on Warwick University's 'Warwick Commission on the Future of Cultural Value', on the media board of the Prince's Foundation for Children and the Arts, and on the advisory group for the Lord Mayor of London's City Music Foundation. He is a Fellow of the Royal Society of Arts, of the Radio Academy, and of the London College of Music; an Honorary Fellow of Trinity Laban Conservatoire of Music and Dance, and of Canterbury Christ Church University; an Honorary Member of the

Royal Northern College of Music, and of the Incorporated Society of Musicians; and a Companion of the Chartered Management Institute. Named 'Commercial Radio Programmer of the Year' in 2008, his work has been honoured by the Sony Radio Academy, the Arqiva Commercial Radio Awards, the New York International Radio Festival, the Grammy Awards and the United Nations. In 2012, he was awarded the Sir Charles Groves Prize for 'his outstanding contribution to British music'. He was appointed an OBE in the 2013 New Year Honours for services to music.

Sam Jackson is the Managing Editor of Classic FM, responsible for the radio station's on-air programming output. Previously, he spent four years as the Executive Producer in charge of all aspects of Classic FM's music policy and programming. He manages the station's large-scale music events, such as Classic FM Live at the Royal Albert Hall, and works closely with Classic FM's network of orchestras across the UK. During his nine years at Classic FM, he has produced many of the station's biggest programmes, working with a range of household-name presenters. Since 2008, he has also been the producer of The Classic FM Hall of Fame, the world's biggest annual poll of classical music tastes. His radio programmes have been honoured at the Sony Radio Academy Awards, the Arqiva Commercial Radio Awards and the New York International Radio Festival. In 2013 alone, Classic FM was named 'UK Radio Brand of the Year' at the Sony Radio Academy Awards and 'Best Classical Format' at the New York International Radio Festival. Sam was named one of the Radio Academy's 'Thirty Under Thirty' for two consecutive years and, in 2012, he was the only person working in radio to be named in the Music Week 30 Under 30. He has a first class degree in music from the University of York. A proficient piano and clarinet player, he is the co-author of *The Classic FM Hall of Fame*. Also published by Elliott & Thompson, it achieved *Sunday Times* bestseller status. Sam also spent four years as a presenter on the children's digital radio station Fun Kids. He is a trustee of the UK radio industry body, the Radio Academy.

INDEX

INDEX

INDEX